CW01640866

Complete Comprehension

Year 2

Contents

Schofield&Sims

Year 2 overview

Introduction

Reading is one of the most important outcomes of a primary school education, and one of the most powerful skills we will ever master, as it is crucial for understanding the world around us. It is no exaggeration to say that the benefits of being an effective reader last a lifetime.

Complete Comprehension is a whole-school programme designed to equip pupils with everything they need to become strong, successful readers. The series, which comprises a book of lesson plans, teaching guidance and photocopiable resources for every year group from Year 1 to Year 6, breaks down the complex process of comprehension into separate **Comprehension skills** (see page 5).

The comprehension skills are signposted throughout the series through the use of child-friendly logos and graphics. Each teaching unit includes a photocopiable **Comprehension text** and a set of **Skills focus questions** that target a single skill, along with detailed guidance to support you, the teacher, to model the relevant skill in context using the **Let's try … questions**.

In addition, a **Skills guide** is provided at the end of this introduction (see page 14). It includes an in-depth **description** of each skill, and explains how the skills relate to each other. It also lists **strategies** to help you develop your pupils' familiarity with each skill and offers advice on how to deal with common difficulties. A selection of resources are also available to download from the Schofield & Sims website (www.schofieldandsims.co.uk/completecomprehension), including a selection of child-friendly **Skills graphics**, which explain the skills in simple terms, and **Skills deskmats**, which function as a reminder of the different skills.

In addition to this skill-specific instruction, **Complete Comprehension** prioritises vocabulary expansion, specifically the pre-teaching of vocabulary, as another prerequisite for successful comprehension. Every teaching unit includes a **Language toolkit**, which contains a set of **Key vocabulary** words from the comprehension text and accompanying activities to boost understanding in advance of reading.

The features outlined above are integrated into each **Complete Comprehension** teaching unit alongside enjoyable activities and discussion opportunities. These have a dual function: first, they promote reading for pleasure; second, they support pupils to engage with the text's features and build their background knowledge by exploring the themes in each text. Children are also encouraged to make comparisons with other texts and to reflect on their personal reactions to the text as readers. See pages 6 to 11 for a complete guide to the teaching unit.

The 18 teaching units in this book are designed to be completed at regular intervals over the course of a year: it is recommended that you work through six units a term, leaving the remaining weeks free to spend on other reading work.

The comprehension skills

Each **Complete Comprehension** teaching unit targets one of the following skills, which are all essential for meaningful reading. In particular, word meaning, retrieval and inference are seen as cornerstones of comprehension, as children must be confident in these areas before they can master the remaining skills.

Key Stage 1 Comprehension skills

Word meaning

Understand the meaning of vocabulary in the text.

This symbol is used to represent word meaning in the teaching units.

- Go to page 14 to read more about word meaning.
- Word meaning is the target skill in Units 5, 15 and 16.

Retrieval

Recall key details from the text.

This symbol is used to represent retrieval in the teaching units.

- Go to page 16 to read more about retrieval.
- Retrieval is the target skill in Units 1, 3, 4, 6, 10, 11, 13 and 17.

Sequencing

Put the main events in the text in order.

This symbol is used to represent sequencing in the teaching units.

- Go to page 18 to read more about sequencing.
- Sequencing is the target skill in Unit 8.

Inference

Use details from the text and background knowledge to make judgements about aspects of the text.

This symbol is used to represent inference in the teaching units.

- Go to page 20 to read more about inference.
- Inference is the target skill in Units 2, 7, 9, 12 and 18.

Prediction

Use details from the text and background knowledge to make plausible predictions based on the text.

This symbol is used to represent prediction in the teaching units.

- Go to page 22 to read more about prediction.
- Prediction is the target skill in Unit 14.

Structure of the teaching unit

Every **Complete Comprehension** teaching unit contains the same four components, which are explained below.

Lesson plan

The first two pages of the teaching unit allow you to see the content of the lesson at a glance. Teaching is divided into five steps to give you the flexibility to make the lesson longer or shorter according to your needs (see **Teaching with *Complete Comprehension***, page 8). Taught as a whole, each unit provides the ideal balance of a holistic reading experience and discrete practice of reading skills.

A short **Introduction** gives a synopsis of the text and highlights links to other texts in the book or to other curriculum subjects.

Teaching is split into five steps.

The **Language toolkit** identifies vocabulary terms for pre-teaching and includes a bank of supporting activities. A selection of phonics focuses are also flagged for optional discussion.

The **Reading list** offers a selection of related texts across a range of genres to encourage comparison and the strengthening of background knowledge.

Skills focus

These pages support you to model the target skill for your class using the **Let's try… questions**, which are also included in the downloadable **Modelling slides** for easy display. The mark schemes for the **Pupil questions**, which the children can attempt after the modelling session, are also found here.

The **Target skill** is clearly signposted.

The **Modelling panel** provides detailed guidance for the **Let's try… questions** on the target skill. These questions are also included in the downloadable **Modelling slides**.

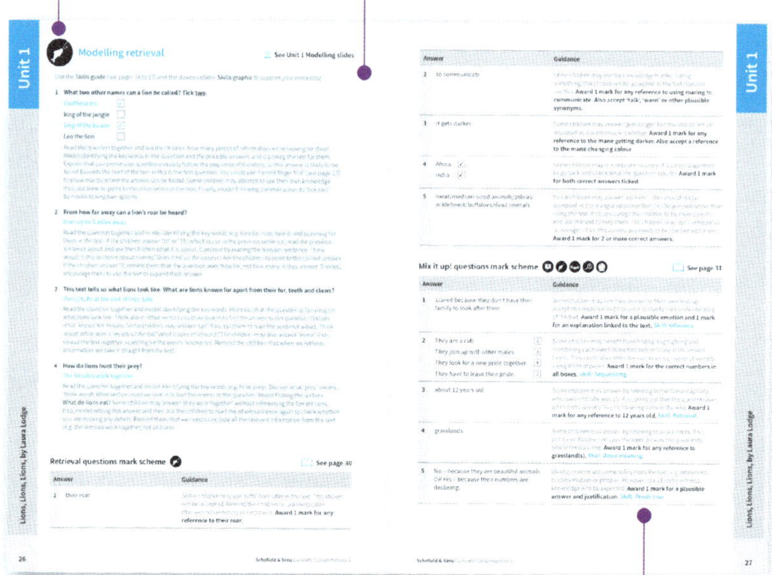

Mark schemes are provided for all pupil questions, and offer guidance on common areas of difficulty.

The final two parts of each unit are aimed at the pupil. These resources may be photocopied for each child.

Comprehension text

The text for each unit is designed to be photocopied, or downloaded and printed, and distributed to each pupil. The lines are widely spaced to allow the children to make their own highlights and annotations.

Each comprehension text is available online in a downloadable format.

A short, child-friendly **Introduction** helps pupils to access the text. This can be read aloud to pupils before reading the text.

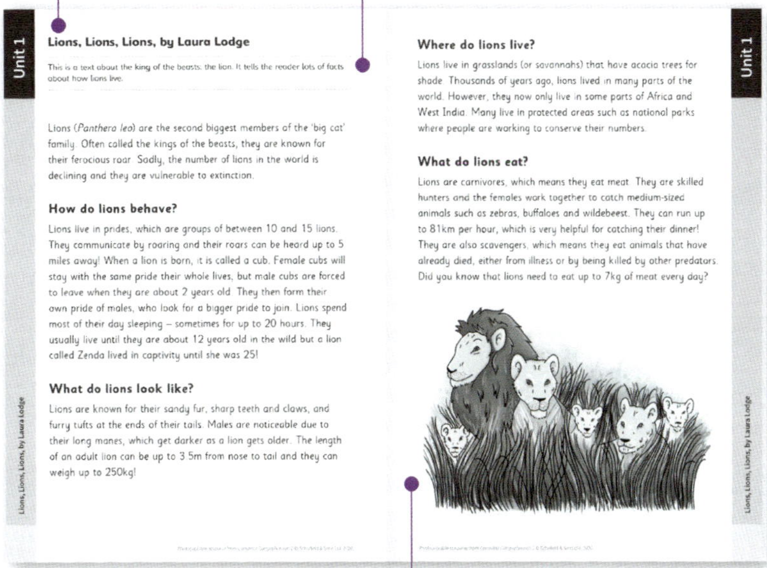

Unit 1

Lions, Lions, Lions, by Laura Lodge

This is a text about the king of the beasts: the lion. It tells the reader lots of facts about how lions live.

Lions (*Panthera leo*) are the second biggest members of the 'big cat' family. Often called the kings of the beasts, they are known for their ferocious roar. Sadly, the number of lions in the world is declining and they are vulnerable to extinction.

How do lions behave?

Lions live in prides, which are groups of between 10 and 15 lions. They communicate by roaring and their roars can be heard up to 5 miles away! When a lion is born, it is called a cub. Female cubs will stay with the same pride their whole lives, but male cubs are forced to leave when they are about 2 years old. They then form their own pride of males, who look for a bigger pride to join. Lions spend most of their day sleeping – sometimes for up to 20 hours. They usually live until they are about 12 years old in the wild but a lion called Zenda lived in captivity until she was 25!

What do lions look like?

Lions are known for their sandy fur, sharp teeth and claws, and furry tufts at the ends of their tails. Males are noticeable due to their long manes, which get darker as a lion gets older. The length of an adult lion can be up to 3.5m from nose to tail and they can weigh up to 250kg!

Where do lions live?

Lions live in grasslands (or savannahs) that have acacia trees for shade. Thousands of years ago, lions lived in many parts of the world. However, they now only live in some parts of Africa and West India. Many live in protected areas such as national parks where people are working to conserve their numbers.

What do lions eat?

Lions are carnivores, which means they eat meat. They are skilled hunters and the females work together to catch medium-sized animals such as zebras, buffaloes and wildebeest. They can run up to 81km per hour, which is very helpful for catching their dinner! They are also scavengers, which means they eat animals that have already died, either from illness or by being killed by other predators. Did you know that lions need to eat up to 7kg of meat every day?

Lions, Lions, Lions, by Laura Lodge

Each text includes at least one **illustration**, which should also be discussed before reading the text.

Pupil resources

Each unit includes a set of five **Target-skill questions** to enable the children to practise applying the target skill, as well as a set of **Mix it up! questions** that offer practice in a range of comprehension skills. The resources can be photocopied for each child.

The **Target skill** is clearly signposted.

The **Mix it up! questions** can be used to practise a range of skills.

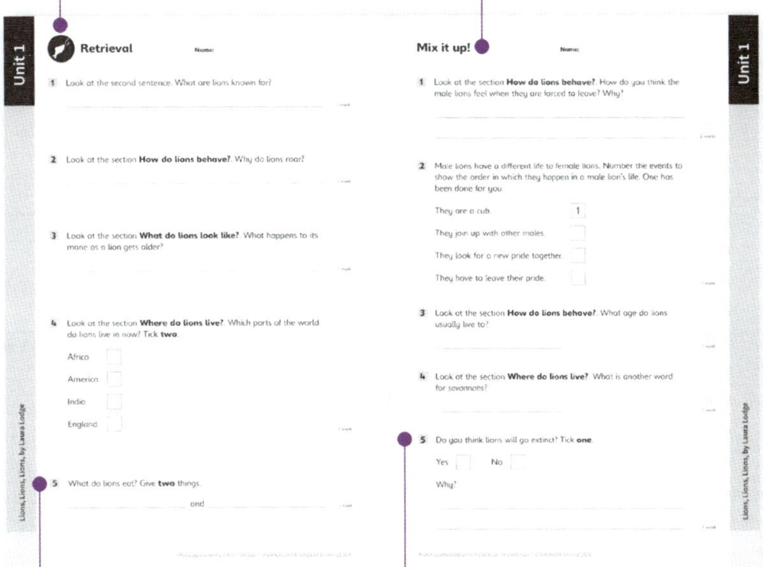

Unit 1

Retrieval Name:

1 Look at the second sentence. What are lions known for?

2 Look at the section **How do lions behave?**. Why do lions roar?

3 Look at the section **What do lions look like?**. What happens to its mane as a lion gets older?

4 Look at the section **Where do lions live?**. Which parts of the world do lions live in now? Tick **two**.

Africa

America

India

England

5 What do lions eat? Give **two** things.

and

Mix it up! Name:

1 Look at the section **How do lions behave?**. How do you think the male lions feel when they are forced to leave? Why?

2 Male lions have a different life to female lions. Number the events to show the order in which they happen in a male lion's life. One has been done for you.

They are a cub. 1

They join up with other males.

They look for a new pride together.

They have to leave their pride.

3 Look at the section **How do lions behave?**. What age do lions usually live to?

4 Look at the section **Where do lions live?**. What is another word for savannahs?

5 Do you think lions will go extinct? Tick **one**.

Yes No

Why?

Lions, Lions, Lions, by Laura Lodge

The **Target-skill questions** can be used to practise the skill after modelling the **Let's try… questions** for your class.

The **Mix-it up! questions** would work well as a homework task, if desired.

Teaching with *Complete Comprehension*

There are 18 teaching units in this book. They can be used flexibly, but it is recommended that they are taught consecutively, as they have been arranged in a specific order to promote discussion and build progression. There are six units to complete each term, leaving the remaining weeks free to spend on other reading work. The teaching units are followed by three optional **Progress checks** (see **Assessment**, page 11).

Each teaching unit is divided into five steps, which are shown in the diagram below. These could be taught as separate sessions over the course of a week; alternatively, multiple steps could easily be combined into a single session.

The **Get ready, First steps** and **Skills focus** steps form the backbone of each teaching unit and should be completed in order. The optional **Explore** and **Where next?** steps are intended to be adapted as necessary to fit the time you have available and the needs of your cohort.

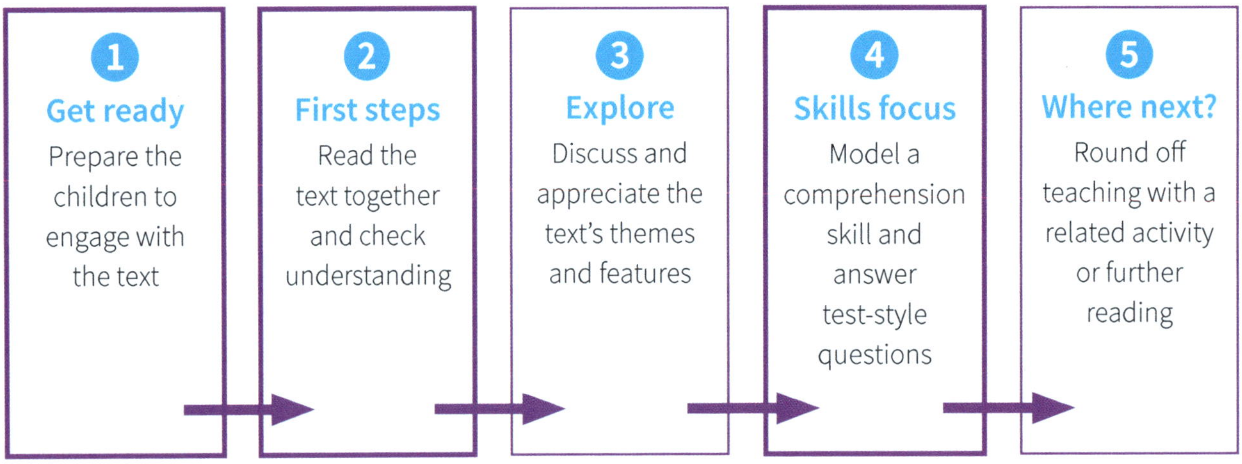

1 Get ready

The **Get ready** session is designed to be carried out verbally as a class.

Start by introducing pupils to the **Key vocabulary** terms in the **Language toolkit**. These are words from the text passage that are unusual or that the children may find difficult to read or understand. Use the **Vocabulary discussion questions** to encourage the children to use the words in context, referring to related or opposite words if desired. You could then use the **Vocabulary activities** to reinforce understanding.

At Key Stage 1, the **Phonics** section of the toolkit also includes a summary of relevant phonics covered in the text passage (e.g. split digraphs; common exception words), providing you with flexible opportunities to discuss recent learning in context. The **Phonics activity** could be used as an enjoyable class challenge to encourage the children to apply their phonics knowledge.

Once your pupils are comfortable with the language in the toolkit, display the comprehension text and accompanying illustration(s) and use the **Get ready questions** to encourage the children to access their existing knowledge of the genre and subject matter. This will ensure that their minds are fully engaged when you come to read the comprehension text together.

In the **Get ready** session, the children will:

- discuss word meanings, linking new meanings to those already known
- draw on what they already know or on background information provided by the teacher
- link what they have read or heard to their own experiences.

2 First steps

Like the **Get ready** session, the **First steps** session is intended to be conducted verbally as a class.

Begin by reading the comprehension text with your class. The **First steps questions**, which should be discussed after reading the text, follow the order of the text and help you to ensure that the children have grasped the basic outline of the passage. The work done in this part of the teaching unit will prepare them to answer more complex questions in the **Skills focus** session (see page 10).

In the **First steps** session, the children will:

- listen to and discuss a wide range of poems, stories and non-fiction
- check that the text makes sense to them as they read, and correct inaccurate reading.

3 Explore

This optional session can be adapted to the needs of your cohort. It offers opportunities for further discussion and enrichment activities to bring the text to life.

The **Explore** discussion questions highlight key themes or literary features of the text. They support the development of analytical skills and encourage the children to express their opinions and listen to the views of their peers, promoting a culture of active reading.

The **Explore** enrichment activities might include using imperative verbs to guide their partner after reading an instructional text. These activities, which represent an enjoyable change of pace within the lesson, will help to build positive attitudes to reading.

In the **Explore** session, the children will:

- learn to appreciate and recite rhymes and poems
- become very familiar with key stories, fairy stories and traditional tales, retelling them and considering their particular characteristics
- participate in discussion of what is read to them, taking turns and listening to what others say.

4 Skills focus

This is the skills-based session of the teaching unit. From Year 2 onwards, the teaching unit is always structured around three sets of questions: modelled target-skill questions (the **Let's try... questions**), practice target-skill questions and mixed skill questions.

1 Model the target skill

First, introduce or recap the target skill, perhaps using one of the downloadable **Skills graphics** to focus the children's attention. The strategies suggested in the relevant pages of the **Skills guide** (see pages 14 to 23) may also be helpful at this point.

Once you have explained the skill, display the **Let's try... questions** (also available as a downloadable resource). Using the answers and modelling guidance provided on the **Skills focus** pages of each unit (see page 6), model the questions for your class. The modelling process is intended to be an interactive experience for the children. The **Modelling panel** contains prompts to help you keep them engaged and highlight the steps in your method.

2 Practise the target skill

Once the **Let's try... questions** have been discussed and completed, the children increase their familiarity with the target skill by working through the **Target-skill questions**. The children could work in small groups to complete these questions, with adult supervision as required. Answers and guidance can be found on the **Skills focus** pages of each teaching unit.

3 Practise a range of comprehension skills

The session ends with a set of **Mix it up! questions**, which offer practice in a range of the Key Stage 1 comprehension skills. These questions are a good way to build the children's confidence in recognising questions from different skill areas. They would also work well as a homework task, if desired.

In the **Skills focus** session, the children will:

- discuss the significance of the title and events
- make inferences on the basis of what is said and done
- predict what might happen on the basis of what has been read so far
- explain clearly their understanding of what is read to them.

5 Where next?

This optional session includes two useful resources that encourage further engagement with the text. The **Reading list** offers a selection of related texts, categorised by genre, which could be used alongside the main unit text to build background knowledge or provide some interesting contrasts. (See **The comprehension texts**, page 12, for guidance on making contrasts between the texts within this book.)

The **Speaking and listening task** and the **Writing task** can be used to help you round off the unit. Both tasks are closely linked to the themes in the comprehension text, and act as a bridge to other areas of the English curriculum. They also represent an opportunity for the children to apply and strengthen the background knowledge they have gained in the course of the teaching unit.

In the **Where next?** session, the children will:

- listen to and discuss a wide range of poems, stories and non-fiction
- develop pleasure in reading and motivation to read.

Assessment

Each **Complete Comprehension** book contains three **Progress checks** designed to be used at the end of each term. These are informal assessments, in which the children work more independently (without the support of the full teaching unit structure) to answer a set of questions that cover a range of comprehension skills. The Progress checks can be used to boost the children's confidence and provide introductory practice for the reading component of the national tests (SATs). They are designed to be used as a helpful transition towards more formal assessment resources. Full marking guidance is provided for each question.

Running the Progress checks

1. Give each child a copy of the comprehension text and spend a few minutes looking at it together, discussing the title and any illustrations. Read the pupil introduction aloud and discuss any questions the children have. You could also consider dividing the text into shorter sections if some children require further scaffolding.
2. Once all the children have read the text, you could briefly remind them of the different comprehension skills they have worked on and discuss how they can identify the questions in each skill area. You may wish to use the downloadable **Skills graphics** or refer to the **Skills guide** (see pages 14 to 23) to help with this. You could also clarify some of the vocabulary that the children have found tricky during reading, but this discussion should be brief.
3. Encourage the children to reread the text before answering the questions independently. There should be no set time allotted to this activity; allow the children to spend as long as they wish on the Progress check and encourage them to review their answers when they have finished. If they find a question challenging, support them to identify the target comprehension skill and provide them with the relevant **Skills graphic** to remind them what they need to consider when thinking about their answer.

Please note that the Progress check is a tool designed to give a brief snapshot of pupils' comprehension. It should not be used as a formal assessment but can give you an indication of areas your class are finding more challenging, which you can then use to guide your teaching.

The comprehension texts

This book contains 21 text passages in total. The texts are arranged in themed pairs, linked by either author or subject matter. These pairings have been planned to facilitate discussion and comparison of related texts as you move through the book. They can be used alongside the external resources in each unit's **Reading list** (see page 10).

In addition to discussing the units in their intended pairs, there are many other links you can make between the texts in each book, including discussing texts of the same genre. As many of the links are cross-curricular, these extra class discussions can be a useful way to strengthen the children's background knowledge. The **Curriculum links chart** below uses shading to show the text pairs and the cross-curricular links for the texts in this book.

Curriculum links in *Complete Comprehension 2*

Unit	Title	Author	Genre	Curriculum links
1	Lions, Lions, Lions	Laura Lodge	Non-fiction *Information text*	Science: Animals, including humans
2	There's a Lion in My Cornflakes	Michelle Robinson	Fiction	
3	The Great Fire of London	Emma Adams	Non-fiction *Narrative non-fiction*	History: Significant events
4	Guy Fawkes	Laura Lodge	Non-fiction *Information text*	History: Significant individuals
5	Eight Candles Burning	Celia Warren	Poetry	PSHE: Communities
6	Christmas Eve	Brian Moses	Poetry *Rhyme*	PSHE: Communities
Progress check 1	Ruby's Worry	Tom Percival	Fiction	PSHE: Describing feelings
7	Perfectly Norman	Tom Percival	Fiction	PSHE: Describing feelings
8	Sir Charlie Stinky Socks: The Really Big Adventure	Kristina Stephenson	Fiction	
9	The Night Dragon	Naomi Howarth	Fiction	

Unit	Title	Author	Genre	Curriculum links
10	How to Build a Gingerbread House	Laura Lodge	Non-fiction *Instructional text*	Mathematics: Measurement
11	Hansel and Gretel	Laura Lodge	Fiction *Traditional tale*	
12	Hansel and Gretel	Bethan Woollvin	Fiction	
Progress check 2	The Life of Roald Dahl: A Marvellous Adventure	Emma Fischel	Non-fiction *Biography*	History: Life in different periods
13	George's Marvellous Medicine	Roald Dahl	Fiction	
14	Horrid Henry and the Football Fiend	Francesca Simon	Fiction	
15	The Hundred-Mile-An-Hour Dog	Jeremy Strong	Fiction	
16	The Darkest Dark	Chris Hadfield	Fiction	Science: Earth and space
17	Dogs in Space	Vix Southgate	Non-fiction *Narrative non-fiction*	Science: Earth and space
18	A Bottle of Happiness	Pippa Goodheart	Fiction	PSHE: Describing feelings
Progress check 3	Ossiri and the Bala Mengro	Richard O'Neill and Katharine Quarmby	Fiction	

Word meaning

See Units 5, 15 and 16

Understanding word meaning

Without an understanding of words, effective reading is impossible. As Lemov (2016)[1] remarked, 'Successful reading relies on a reader's capacity to understand both a large number of words as well as the subtleties and nuances of those words, even when words change their meaning according to the setting.' Learning to define words in context is an important skill, and one that confident readers use regularly.

It is crucial that children do not simply learn to 'define' individual words, like a dictionary, but that they understand the vocabulary they encounter in the context in which it appears. The National Curriculum (2014) requires children in Key Stage 1 to understand texts by 'drawing on what they already know or on background information or vocabulary provided by the teacher', while children in Key Stage 2 must check that a text makes sense to them by 'explaining the meaning of words in context'. Developing this skill helps children to make links between known and unknown words and teaches them to use the context of a word to interpret its meaning.

Word meaning in *Complete Comprehension*

The teaching of vocabulary can be divided into two key types: explicit and implicit instruction.[2]

Explicit instruction is the teaching of specific words and phrases that are necessary to either comprehend a specific text or comprehend meaning more generally *in advance of reading*.

Implicit instruction is the teaching of strategies that help learners assess their understanding of words *as they read*.

Word meaning is the target skill of several teaching units in each **Complete Comprehension** book. In addition, both types of vocabulary instruction are addressed in every teaching unit: explicit instruction is the focus of the **Get ready** session, in which **Key vocabulary** terms are taught before reading the comprehension passage. Implicit instruction underlies the work done in the subsequent **Explore** and **Skills focus** sessions (see pages 8 to 11 for a full description of the teaching sequence).

Word meaning questions usually require children to make links between synonyms. In **Complete Comprehension**, questions may be worded as follows:

- Which word is closest in meaning to … ? Tick **one**.
- Explain what the word(s) … tell(s) you about… .
- What does the word … mean in this sentence/line?
- Underline the word which tells you that… .
- Draw lines to match each word to its meaning.
- Find and copy **one** word/a group of words that means the same as… .

Often, questions that assess the skill of word meaning only require the child to find out one piece of information. However, this information does not usually come directly from the text but must be deduced using vocabulary knowledge. Word meaning questions thus sometimes require the use of other comprehension skills, such as inference (see page 20) to reach the correct answer.

Key challenges

As they read, many children skip over words they do not understand, losing meaning in the process. Teaching children to note down and ask about any vocabulary they do not understand when reading is therefore crucial.

Many children have relatively shallow vocabulary knowledge, only understanding a word when it appears in a familiar context. For example, many will have no trouble with 'It was *raining*' but will struggle with 'The money was *raining down*'. It is important to provide opportunities for children to deepen their knowledge by investigating words in a range of contexts.

Children with less secure vocabularies may also struggle to generate linked vocabulary (e.g. knowing that 'repeat', 'redo' and 'recycle' are all connected by the prefix 're–', which refers to doing something again). Incorporating the etymology and categorisation strategies described on page 15 when you are teaching will support the children to make these connections.

Strategies for developing word meaning

- **Context clues:** Reading around the target word or sentence to gain a general idea of the context can help children make an educated guess about the word's meaning. However, it is important to note that using context clues can also lead to confusion, as authors generally do not write with the primary aim of supporting readers to make meaning. When you use this strategy, the children should only be directed to words with a helpful context. When teaching vocabulary explicitly, it is a good idea to introduce a new word within multiple contexts before modelling how to use the specific context to construct meaning. The vocabulary discussion questions in each unit's **Language toolkit** (see page 6) help the children to understand the **Key vocabulary** terms in context.

- **Substitution:** Encourage the children to make substitutions to help them check the meaning of a word. If the target word is replaced by a new word, does the sentence still make sense? Is the new word a synonym, or has the meaning of the sentence changed? If the sentence still 'works', how does this information help the children to answer the question?

- **Shades of meaning:** When the children are investigating possible synonyms for unfamiliar vocabulary, ensure that they understand that a synonym is similar to, but not the same as, the original word. Asking the children to place a group of synonyms on a scale from the weakest to the strongest can help them to appreciate nuances.

- **Categorisation:** For vocabulary knowledge to become deeper and more securely embedded, the children need to be able to categorise vocabulary. For example, knowing that 'zebra' and 'mongoose' both refer to animals, and that 'angry' and 'exasperated' both describe negative feelings, will support the children to make essential links as they read. Providing them with word cards to sort into categories can help to build up this understanding.

- **Etymology:** Children need to be taught the meanings of root words, prefixes and suffixes, and should be encouraged to use these to help them make educated guesses about word meaning. Throughout **Complete Comprehension**, and especially at Key Stage 2, etymology activities are included in the **Vocabulary activities** section of the **Language toolkit**.

Modelling word meaning

When modelling word meaning for your class using the **Let's try… questions** (see page 6), the steps below may be useful. Specific modelling guidance is also provided in the relevant teaching units.

1. Read aloud. Model reading the whole question carefully.
2. Identify and underline the key words in the question.
3. Model scanning the text efficiently to locate each key word, or related key words, from the question.
4. Demonstrate reading the sentences before and after each key word to look for context clues.
5. Make links aloud between the key words and their synonyms. Model using this knowledge to help you gauge the meaning.
6. Formulate an answer. Model checking that it answers the question.

1 Lemov, D. (2016) *Reading Reconsidered*. San Francisco: Jossey Bass, p. 251.

2 Lemov (2016), pp. 253–256.

Retrieval

See Units 1, 3, 4, 6, 10, 11, 13 and 17

Understanding retrieval

Retrieval is the act of efficiently locating, and reproducing, important details in a text. Other reading skills cannot be mastered without a knowledge of retrieval, which is often seen as the most important reading skill.

The National Curriculum (2014) requires children in Key Stage 1 to 'identify/explain key aspects of fiction and non-fiction texts', while children in Key Stage 2 must 'retrieve and record information/identify key details from fiction and non-fiction'. Strong retrieval skills are essential for effective comprehension.

Retrieval in *Complete Comprehension*

Retrieval relies on a secure understanding of the information in a text. The key to successful retrieval is remembering that the information required to answer the question is always stated explicitly in the text. The children must be encouraged to focus on the text rather than relying on memory or on their extrinsic knowledge (in contrast to other comprehension skills, such as inference – see page 20).

Because it is so important, retrieval is the focus skill in many of the units in each **Complete Comprehension** book. This allows the children to practise retrieval in many different contexts. In addition, further retrieval practice is built into every teaching unit through the questions in the **First steps** session (see page 9) of the lesson. These straightforward questions encourage the children to develop the habit of looking back at the text after their initial reading to pick out key details. This helps them to generate a 'mental model' of the text, which will give them a better idea of where to look for answers when they encounter more formal questions in the **Skills focus** session (see page 6).

In **Complete Comprehension**, retrieval questions often begin with a 'question word', such as 'who', 'what', 'where', 'when', 'how' or 'which', that relates to the target information (e.g. 'who' for a character; 'when' for a time). Often, some of the words used in retrieval questions are taken from the text, which provides an important signpost to readers of where in the text the answer is likely to be found. The children should be encouraged to pay attention to the number of details they have been asked to give, as retrieval questions will often ask for more than one piece of information.

In **Complete Comprehension**, retrieval questions are often worded as follows:

- Who.../What.../When.../ Where.../How.../ Which...?
- Give **two**...
- According to the text...
- Find and copy **two** examples of ... from the text.
- Draw lines to match each statement...
- Tick to show whether the statement is true or false.
- Tick to show whether the statement(s) below is/are fact or opinion.

It is important to note that retrieval questions will sometimes require the children to draw on other comprehension skills, such as inference (see page 20), to reach the correct answer.

Key challenges

Some children find retrieval difficult; they try to remember the information or use their extrinsic knowledge to answer questions, instead of referring back to the text. When teaching retrieval, you must emphasise the fact that the information will always be found in the text.

Strategies for developing retrieval

- **Identify key words:** To retrieve information, the children need to be able to identify key words in the question before locating them in the text. This should be modelled explicitly by looking at the question, removing any extraneous information, and then deciding on the key words needed. Sometimes, the key words in the question will be synonymous with words in the text. It is important to model discussing possible synonyms that the text may use instead of the key words.
- **Scanning:** Scanning is the process of rapidly searching the text for specific information, such as a key word. This is a fundamental reading skill that should be prioritised and practised. It is important to model a systematic approach by scanning every line of the text, perhaps using your finger or a ruler on the page. Activities that do not require the children to decode may be helpful for developing scanning skills. The children could use 'search and find' texts, such as the *Where's Wally?* books, to practise scanning. Alternatively, you could provide a section of text and challenge the children to see how many words, letter strings or punctuation marks they can find in it within a given time.
- **Point out the evidence/Fastest finger first:** To emphasise the importance of always referring to the text rather than falling back on extrinsic knowledge, challenge the children to 'point out the evidence' for their answer, for example by highlighting, circling or underlining the text. You could also play games such as 'Fastest finger first', in which players race to physically place their finger on the word(s) in the text that answer a question or provide a relevant detail.

Modelling retrieval

When modelling retrieval for your class using the **Let's try... questions** (see page 6), the steps below may be useful. Specific modelling guidance is also provided in the relevant teaching units.

1. Read the question aloud. Remind the children that they should resist the temptation to draw conclusions based on their own knowledge, and model focusing your attention back to the words in the text.
2. Locate the key words in your concept or question.
3. Scan the text for those key words, or related key words, and highlight or underline them.
4. If necessary, read around the key words to look for context clues.
5. Find the information you need in the text and highlight or underline it.
6. Check that the information you have found answers the question.

Sequencing

See Unit 8

Understanding sequencing

Sequencing is the act of ordering the events or information in a text. Although this may sound straightforward, sequencing is a complex skill that relies on a secure understanding of the whole text. Children must be able to retrieve key details from the text and then use this information to work out the chronology of events, alternating between focusing on sections of the text and the text as a whole. Sequencing is important for reading longer texts and for understanding the whole of a text. The National Curriculum (2014) requires children in Key Stage 1 to discuss 'the sequence of events in books and how items of information are related'. Almost every other reading skill requires the ability to sequence and retell the events and information in a text. As with the skill of retrieval (see page 16), the key to successful sequencing is to use evidence from the whole text, rather than relying on memory.

Sequencing in *Complete Comprehension*

Sequencing is the focus skill for a number of units in the **Complete Comprehension** books aimed at children in Key Stage 1. Additional sequencing practice is also built into every unit through the **First steps** session (see page 9). The **First steps** questions, which encourage children to recall the most important points from the text, are in chronological order: this helps the children to generate a 'mental model' of the text and develop a better idea of the sequence of events in the text as a whole.

In **Complete Comprehension**, the skill of sequencing is often assessed using a 'sequencing statements' format, in which children are asked to write numbers in boxes next to a list of four or five sentences to show the order in which events from the text happened, as in the example below:

Number the events to show the order in which they happened in the story.

The wolf tried to get the three little pigs.	2
The pigs built their own houses.	1
The pigs lived happily ever after.	4
The wolf ran away.	3

Sequencing questions also often begin with a 'question word', such as 'who', 'what', 'when' or 'which', that relates to the target information (e.g. 'who' for a character, 'when' for a time). Often, some of the words used in sequencing questions are taken from the text, which provides an important signpost to readers of where in the text the answer is likely to be found. In **Complete Comprehension**, sequencing questions may be worded as follows:

- Think about the whole story…
- Sort these…
- Which of these events happened first? Tick **one**.
- What did … do first/before/after/as soon as … ?
- When in the story did…?
- Look at the first/second/third paragraph. Which event happened first/last? Tick **one**.

Key challenges

Sequencing requires a secure understanding of the text and a good working memory. Children sometimes struggle to sequence information from a text because they cannot keep track of all of its constituent parts. This is because sequencing carries a high cognitive load – readers have to decode and retrieve information, then rely on their working memory to order that information. They must then use their knowledge of time adverbs and conjunctions to understand what they are being asked to do and respond appropriately to the sequencing activity.

Strategies for developing sequencing

- **Simplified sequencing:** You could reduce the cognitive load of sequencing by using images to represent events in a text, or by reducing the number of statements that the children need to sequence.
- **Sequencing vocabulary:** To answer sequencing questions, the children need to understand the relevant vocabulary. It is important to discuss and draw attention to sequencing language such as 'first', 'after', 'next', 'finally' and 'once upon a time' as you read, both in English lessons and across the curriculum.
- **Physical sequencing:** Sometimes children struggle to sequence large chunks of text. If this is the case, separate the text into sections and then cut those sections up, modelling your thinking process as you physically order and sequence the parts of the text. This is especially useful when modelling how to answer a 'sequencing statements' question.
- **Skim-reading:** Skim-reading means reading a text quickly to assimilate the main ideas. It enables children to gain an overview of what each section of a text is about. This helps them to create a mental map of the text and to predict where information is most likely to be found. This strategy is particularly helpful when reading non-fiction. You could introduce skim-reading by showing the children the text with most lines blacked out, so that only the title and first sentence of each paragraph are visible. Discuss what this content tells the reader about the paragraph or section. Encourage the children to use the first line of a paragraph to 'get the gist' of the text before reading it in more detail. It is also worth reminding them to look at titles, subheadings, illustrations, captions and any words that are formatted in bold or italics.
- **Graphic organisers:** The children may benefit from using a graphic organiser to support their sequencing of a text. It is important to explicitly model your thought process as you demonstrate these strategies. Examples of useful graphic organisers include:
  - Story maps: The children map out the main events in a text by drawing pictures that represent the key points and linking these using arrows.
  - Storyboards: The children draw six key events from the story and write captions for them.
  - Timelines: The children put the key events of the story into chronological order.
  - Beginning, middle, end: The children draw or write the main event for the beginning, middle and end of the text.
  - Story mountains: The children write the key events of the story using the following headings to structure their ideas: 'beginning', 'build-up', 'problem', 'resolution' and 'ending'.

Modelling sequencing

When modelling sequencing for your class using the **Let's try… questions** (see page 6), the steps below may be useful. Specific modelling guidance can also be found in the relevant teaching units.

1. Read the question aloud. Tell the children they must use the text when they sequence, rather than relying on their memory.
2. Locate the information you need to sequence. Model identifying whether you are sequencing multiple points or one point.
3. Skim-read the text to locate the relevant point(s) for sequencing. Highlight or underline each point.
4. Model ordering the information.
5. Check that the information you have ordered answers the question.

Inference

See Units 2, 7, 9, 12 and 18

Understanding inference

Inference skills are essential for understanding our world: we use them whenever we gauge other people's emotions using their facial expressions or tone of voice. Children will therefore have some ability to infer even before they learn to decode.

Inference is often described as the ability to 'read between the lines' or 'find clues' in a text. However, it can be more helpfully defined as the skill of using both evidence from the text and our background knowledge to come to a reasonable conclusion.

Academics have separated inference-making into a number of distinct categories (Kispal, 2008).[3] However, most recognise two main categories of inference:

Coherence inferences are necessary for basic comprehension. They can be formulated from understanding a text's cohesive devices, such as pronouns, or from linking background knowledge to the text. For example, from the sentence 'Maggie loved playing catch but sometimes she refused to bring the ball back', we could infer that 'Maggie', 'she' and 'her' are the same (using cohesive devices), and that Maggie is probably a dog (using background knowledge).

Elaborative inferences are not necessary for basic comprehension, but they make a text more interesting. An elaborative inference might be a prediction or speculation that the reader makes about a character or the consequences of an action. For example, from the sentence 'Maggie loved playing catch but sometimes she refused to give the ball back to her owner', we could infer that, because she sometimes refused to bring back the ball, Maggie might be a puppy. Elaborative inferences depend on background knowledge and are thus more demanding than coherence inferences.

The National Curriculum (2014) requires pupils in Key Stage 1 to be 'making inferences on the basis of what is being said and done'. At Key Stage 2, learners must rely on their background knowledge, 'drawing inferences such as inferring characters' feelings, thoughts and motives'.

Inference in *Complete Comprehension*

Inference is the focus skill in a high proportion of the units in each **Complete Comprehension** book, to allow the children to practise inference in different contexts.

In **Complete Comprehension**, inference questions often include the phrase 'How/Why do you think…'. It is a good idea to draw the children's attention to this wording to help them remember that they need to make a judgement using their own knowledge *in addition to* the text, rather than limiting themselves to details explicitly mentioned in the text, as they would when answering a retrieval (see page 16) or sequencing (see page 18) question. Once the children's inference skills have begun to embed, some questions will require them to provide evidence to support their inferences. You should explore the expectations of these questions with the children.

In **Complete Comprehension**, inference questions are often worded as follows:

- Why…/How…/Which…?
- Why/How/What do you think…? Explain your answer.
- How can you tell…?
- Explain why…
- Give two reasons…
- True or false…
- Think about the whole text. What impression do you get of … ? Give **one** impression and **one** piece of evidence.

It is important to note that inference questions always require the use of other comprehension skills, such as retrieval (see page 16), to reach the correct answer.

Key challenges

For many children, inference is a real challenge. This is because they are required to make an intuitive leap to move from what they *know* (direct evidence that they can see in the text) to what they *think* (the conclusion they come to after locating and assessing the evidence). An understanding of the text, robust vocabulary skills and strong background knowledge are essential prerequisites for successful inference-making. The skills of word meaning (see page 14) and retrieval (see page 16) must therefore be embedded before inference skills can fully develop.

Strategies for developing inference

- **Think-alouds:** Confident readers make inferences automatically as they read. However, when teaching children to infer, you should slow down and model your thought process. 'Think-alouds' (statements that verbalise your thought process) can be useful. For example, you could think aloud to model dividing your thoughts into two types: 'what I know' and 'what I think' (e.g. 'From the text, I know that... This makes me think...'). Think-alouds can also be used to model refining an inference (e.g. 'I thought that... because... but... so...'), and can be incorporated into the strategies below.
- **Inference check:** Marzano (2010)[4] suggested that teachers could support inference-making by modelling asking the following four questions:

  1 'What is my inference?'

  2 'What did I use to make my inference?'

  3 'How good was my thinking?'

  4 'Do I need to change my thinking?'

  These questions could be used in the strategy above.
- **Objects and visual representations:** Using objects and images that relate to the text can be helpful when exploring inference, as this eliminates the need to decode and therefore reduces cognitive load. You could use images to represent characters or scenes from the text, and model inference by adding thought or speech bubbles to them. Alternatively, you could assign objects to characters from a text. For example, if you were reading 'The Three Bears', you could provide different porridge bowls and ask the children to decide which character each bowl is most likely to belong to.
- **Real-life scenarios:** Many children will need prompting to connect the inferences they make in everyday life with inferences made while reading. One strategy is to use models such as 'think-alouds' to explore real-life scenarios, using clues to make inferences about people's preferences, location or relationship. For instance, you could listen to a conversation or watch a video clip showing two people and ask the children what they can infer about their relationship (e.g. 'Do you think these people are friends or enemies? How can you tell from what they do and what they say?').
- **Graphic organisers:** These are especially helpful when the children are asked to provide evidence or an explanation for their inferences. For example, the children could complete a 'I can see...I know...I think' chart: a table with three columns in which they first record what they can see in the text or image. They then record what they know from the text, and use this to write what they think (the inference). It is important to explicitly model the thinking process behind this strategy.

Modelling inference

When modelling the skill of inference for your class using the **Let's try... questions** (see page 6), the steps below may be useful. Specific modelling guidance is also provided in the teaching units.

1 Read the question aloud.

2 Locate the key words in the question. Scan the text for those key words, or related key words, and highlight or underline them.

3 Read around the key words to look for context clues.

4 Discuss what the text tells you about the key words.

5 Model using this information to make an inference. This might involve relating the ideas in the question to your own experiences to model the use of background knowledge.

6 Model justifying your inference with evidence from the text.

7 Check that the information answers the question.

---

3 Kispal, A. (2008) Effective Teaching of Inference Skills for Reading. *Literature Review*. Research Report DCSF-RR031, National Foundation for Educational Research.

4 Marzano, R.J. (2010) The Art and Science of Teaching/Teaching Inference *Educational Leadership*, 67(7), pp80–81.

Prediction

See Unit 14

Understanding prediction

Prediction is the skill of being able to make inferences (see page 20) about what is likely to happen later in a text. In a fiction extract, this might relate to a character's actions; in a non-fiction extract, it might be about the type of information that will be found in the next part of the text. A skilled reader makes predictions automatically, finding links between known and new information as they read. The National Curriculum (2014) requires pupils in Key Stage 1 to predict 'what might happen on the basis of what has been read so far' while Key Stage 2 children need to predict 'what might happen from details stated and implied'. The ability to make predictions requires a thorough understanding of a passage. To make a plausible prediction, the reader must be able to select details from the text and use these, and their own background knowledge, to decide what is likely to happen.

Prediction in *Complete Comprehension*

One teaching unit in each **Complete Comprehension** book focuses on prediction. In addition, the children's prediction skills are engaged in the **Get ready** session of every unit. These questions encourage the children to use the title and any subheadings, illustration(s) and their own background knowledge to help them predict what a passage will be about. Following on from this, the **Mix it up! questions** in the **Skills focus** session offer frequent opportunities to practise and refine this important skill. (See pages 6 to 11 for a complete guide to the teaching unit.)

As prediction requires the use of inference skills, it is not surprising that prediction questions are often worded similarly to inference questions. Once the children's prediction skills have begun to embed, they will often be asked to justify their predictions using the text. In **Complete Comprehension**, prediction questions may be worded as follows:

- Who.../What.../When.../Where.../How.../Which...?
- Predict...
- Imagine...
- Which is most likely...?

The skill of prediction is usually assessed through tick-box or extended response questions: however, on occasion, it may also be assessed through other question types, which may require additional teacher modelling.

Key challenges

Often, children with poor comprehension skills will be able to formulate a prediction, but their predictions will not be sufficiently plausible, and may not be linked to the original text. You should remind all children to use the text to inform any prediction and underlying inference; this can also help when answering prediction questions that require additional justification, which can be challenging. (For more information on the challenges of teaching and using inference, see page 20.)

Strategies for developing prediction

- **'Think-alouds':** One way to support children to predict is to use 'think-alouds' (statements that verbalise your thought process). You can use think-alouds at different points to model prediction:
  - Before reading (e.g. 'I've found this book and when I look at the title/illustrations I think... because... so that might mean... I could predict...').
  - While reading (e.g. 'I wonder what's going to happen next. I know... So that makes me think... I could predict...').
  - After reading (e.g. 'While I was reading I predicted... I was right because/I was incorrect because...').
- **Multiple predictions:** Confident readers not only make predictions, but they also constantly re-evaluate and adjust their predictions as they read. One way to help the children develop this skill is to start from a narrow viewpoint: for example, you could show them a small part of an illustration or a phrase from the text and ask them make a prediction based on what they can see, then show them more of the picture/text and ask them to make another prediction. This will help them to adjust their first prediction as they read.

- **Making links:** Making plausible predictions involves making links to other known texts, characters and information. Although predictions should be made with reference to a specific text, extrinsic knowledge relating to the wider genre or subject matter of the text is also important. For instance, if you are reading 'Cinderella' with your class and the children have read other fairy tales, they will know that in a fairy tale the main character usually lives happily ever after, and this could have a bearing on any predictions they make. As part of the 'think-aloud' process detailed above, you could model making links to known texts and different types of text. In **Complete Comprehension**, each extract has at least one linked text; listed on pages 12 to 13 and often referred to in the each unit's introduction, these links are designed to help you make connections with the children's existing knowledge. Each unit also includes a **Reading list** of related texts.
- **Graphic organisers:** Once the children have started to make predictions, you could use graphic organisers to help them organise their ideas and scaffold their justifications. It is important to explicitly model the thinking process behind this strategy. Examples of useful graphic organisers for prediction include:
    - 'I predict… because': The children complete a chart that asks them to record their predictions and their justification.
    - 'What has happened… What will happen… What actually happened': The children complete a chart by recording event(s) from the text and their predictions about what will happen next. You could then give them copies of the source text and allow them to read beyond the extract and record what actually happened.

Modelling prediction

When modelling the skill of prediction for your class using the **Let's try… questions** (see page 6), the steps below may be useful. Specific modelling guidance is also provided in the teaching units.

1. Read the question aloud. Point out the need to look back at the text rather than making a hasty prediction that does not relate closely enough to the text – the children need to think about what is *likely* to happen rather than what they *want* to happen.
2. Locate the key words in the question. Scan the text for those key words, or related key words, and highlight or underline them.
3. Read around the key words to look for context clues.
4. Discuss what you know already.
5. Discuss what you think may happen next, linking this back to the text.
6. Model justifying your prediction. This might involve relating the ideas in the question to your own experiences to model using your background knowledge.
7. Check that the information in your answer matches the question.

Lions, Lions, Lions

by Laura Lodge

Printable text • Modelling slides   Photocopiable text and questions • pages 28 to 31

Lions are one of the most recognisable wild animals and one that children will often name first when asked. This text summarises some information about lions in an easy-to-understand report format with clear subheadings. The children will probably already know a few basic facts about lions, but this interesting text should engage them and make them want to find out more. This unit is linked to Unit 2, which features a fictional lion. After completing both units, you may wish to compare the two texts.

1 Get ready

Discuss the **Key vocabulary** identified in the **Language toolkit** and then complete the vocabulary and phonics activities as desired. Please note that the selected vocabulary is a guide. Depending on the needs of your cohort, additional vocabulary discussion may be beneficial before, during and after reading. Next, display the text (pages 28 to 29) so the children can see the title and any illustrations, and encourage the children to discuss the following questions before reading.

1 What type of text is this? How do you know?
An information text/non-fiction. Answers will vary regarding 'How do you know?' (e.g. *I know this because it tells us facts about lions.* Some children may refer to the subheadings; these will be discussed in **First steps**).

2 What do you already know about lions?
Answers will vary, though it is likely that discussion will focus on basic facts about lions (e.g. *they have manes; they live in Africa; they roar*).

3 Have you read any other books about lions?
Answers will vary but should link to other texts the children have read. You may wish to encourage the children to think about both non-fiction and fiction.

4 What is one new thing you would like to find out about lions from this text?
Answers will vary. Try to come back to this question during **Explore** on page 25. At that point, you could ask the children whether the text taught them any of the new things they were hoping to find out.

Language toolkit

Key vocabulary

conserve	declining	extinction
ferocious	skilled	vulnerable

Vocabulary discussion questions

- What is the difference between a **ferocious** lion and a friendly one?
- Which animals are at risk of **extinction**? What can we do to **conserve** them?
- What are you **skilled** at?

Vocabulary activities

1 Encourage the children to pretend to be **ferocious** lions.

2 Use one of the vocabulary activities on page 15 to investigate some of the key words above.

Phonics

Decoding support words	acacia, communicate, ferocious, national, noticeable, scavengers
High frequency words	Decodable: about, by, day, old, very Tricky: called, people, there
Common exception words	every, grass, many, most, old, only, our, people, who, whole, wild

Phonics activity

How many words can the children spot that have the split digraph 'a–e'?

2 First steps

Read the text together and then encourage the children to discuss the following questions.

1 **What was your favourite fact you learnt about lions from the text? Why?**
Answers will vary. Ensure the children explain their opinions using the text.

2 **[Point to the first subheading.] What is this called?**
It is a subheading. The children may call it a title or a heading instead. Ask the children to point to each subheading in turn. You could point out the main text heading to highlight the difference.

3 **The first subheading is about how lions behave. What information does this section give us?**
Answers will vary but should be found within this section only. Encourage the children to use their own words (e.g. *what lions do; who they live with; what their families are like; what their babies are called*).

4 **In which section would I find information about the food that lions like best?**
*In the **What do lions eat?** section.*

5 **Did you like the text? Why? Why not?**
Answers will vary but encourage the children to explain their answers (e.g. *I liked it because it told me lots of new facts*).

3 Explore

- Compare the text to another example of a non-fiction text about lions (you may want to use the **Reading list** suggestions). Discuss the similarities and differences. Are there any features the children could add to make the unit text more engaging or useful (e.g. illustrations, diagrams, tables, photographs, glossary)? The children could work together in groups to improve sections of the text and present these to the class.
- Watch a video clip of lions. Together, compare this with the text – does it match? If it is different, discuss what they might want to find out more about and which section of the text they could add this to.
- Discuss where else lions live apart from in the wild (try to elicit zoos/animal sanctuaries). Have the children ever been to a zoo? What are the children's feelings about zoos? Discuss their opinions together.

4 Skills focus

See pages 26 to 27

Use the information from the **Skills guide** and the relevant **Skills graphic** to introduce the skill of retrieval.

1 Model the skill using the **Unit 1 Modelling slides** and the **Modelling retrieval** guidance on page 26.

2 The children can then attempt the **Retrieval** questions on page 30.

3 Finally, the **Mix it up!** questions on page 31 offer practice in a range of comprehension skills.

Answers and marking guidance for all questions are included on pages 26 to 27.

5 Where next?

- Speaking and listening task: Model using the text to draw an illustration of a pride of lions in their natural habitat. The children could work independently or in pairs to draw their own illustrations, using only the information in the text. They could then verbally compare their drawings with each other, as well as looking at further illustrations of lions, discussing their similarities and differences.
- Writing task: The children could create their own 'Look after the lions' posters to encourage conservation and avoid extinction. They could also find out about other animals that are vulnerable to extinction.

Reading list

Fiction
- *How to be a Lion* by Ed Vere
- *There's a Lion in My Cornflakes* by Michelle Robinson (Linked text: Unit 2)

Class reads
- *We're Going on a Lion Hunt* by David Axtell

Non-fiction
- *National Geographic Kids Readers: Lions* by Laura Marsh

Poetry
- *The Bad Child's Book of Beasts* by Hilaire Belloc
- *National Geographic Book of Animal Poetry* by J. Patrick Lewis

Films
- *The Wild* (Walt Disney Pictures, 2006)

TV series
- *The Zoo* (BBC, 2017–)

Modelling retrieval

See Unit 1 Modelling slides

Use the **Skills guide** (see pages 16 to 17) and the downloadable **Skills graphic** to support your modelling.

1 What two other names can a lion be called? Tick two.

Panthera leo ☑

king of the jungle ☐

king of the beasts ☑

Leo the lion ☐

Read the question together and ask the children how many pieces of information we're looking for (two). Model identifying the key words in the question and the possible answers and scanning the text for them. Explain that comprehension questions usually follow the sequence of the story, so this answer is likely to be found towards the start of the text as this is the first question. You could use 'Fastest finger first' (see page 17) to show exactly where the answer can be found. Some children may attempt to use their own knowledge. If so, ask them to point to the information in the text. Finally, model following the instruction to 'tick two' by model ticking two options.

2 From how far away can a lion's roar be heard?

from up to 5 miles away

Read the question together and model identifying the key words (e.g. how far, roar, heard) and scanning for them in the text. If the children answer '10' or '15', which occur in the previous sentence, read the previous sentence aloud and ask the children what it is about. Continue by reading the relevant sentence. Think aloud: *Is this sentence about roaring? Does it tell us the answer?* Ask the children to point to the correct answer. If the children answer '5', remind them that the question asks 'how far', not how many. If they answer '5 miles', encourage them to use the text to expand their answer.

3 This text tells us what lions look like. What are lions known for apart from their fur, teeth and claws?

(furry) tufts at the end of their tails

Read the question together and model identifying the key words. Point out that the question is focusing on what lions look like. Think aloud: *What section could we look in to find the answer to this question?* Discuss what 'known for' means. Some children may answer 'tail'. If so, ask them to read the sentence aloud. Think aloud: *What does it say about the tail? What is special about it?* The children may also answer 'mane'. If so, reread the text together, scanning for the words 'known for'. Remind the children that when we retrieve information, we take it straight from the text.

4 How do lions hunt their prey?

The females work together.

Read the question together and model identifying the key words (e.g. how, prey). Discuss what 'prey' means. Think aloud: *What section could we look in to find the answer to this question?* Model finding the section **What do lions eat?** Some children may answer 'they work together' without referencing the female lions. If so, model writing this answer and then ask the children to read the whole sentence again to check whether you are missing any details. Remind them that we need to include all the relevant information from the text (e.g. the females work together, not all lions).

Retrieval questions mark scheme

See page 30

Answer	Guidance
1 their roar	Some children may use 'tufts' from later in the text. This should not be accepted. Remind the children to use the locator (the second sentence) to help them. **Award 1 mark for any reference to their roar.**

Answer		Guidance
2	to communicate	Some children may use their knowledge to infer scaring something; this should not be accepted as the text does not say this. **Award 1 mark for any reference to using roaring to communicate. Also accept 'talk', 'warn' or other plausible synonyms.**
3	It gets darker.	Some children may answer 'gets longer' but this should not be accepted as it is extrinsic knowledge. **Award 1 mark for any reference to the mane getting darker. Also accept a reference to the mane changing colour.**
4	Africa ✓ India ✓	Some children may tick only one country. If so, encourage them to go back and check what the question asks for. **Award 1 mark for both correct answers ticked.**
5	meat/medium-sized animals/zebras/wildebeest/buffaloes/dead animals	Some children may answer 'animals' – this should not be accepted as it is a vague response that can be guessed rather than using the text. If so, encourage the children to be more specific and use the text to help them. The children may use 'carnivore' or 'scavenger'; if so, this vocabulary needs to be clarified with them. **Award 1 mark for 2 or more correct answers.**

Mix it up! questions mark scheme

See page 31

Answer		Guidance
1	scared because they don't have their family to look after them	Some children may link their answer to their own feelings – accept this response but discuss it to clarify their understanding of the text. **Award 1 mark for a plausible emotion and 1 mark for an explanation linked to the text.** Skill: Inference.
2	They are a cub. 1 They join up with other males. 3 They look for a new pride together. 4 They have to leave their pride. 2	Some children may benefit from finding, highlighting and numbering each event in the text before filling in the answer boxes. They could also order the events as a group or physically, using strips of paper. **Award 1 mark for the correct numbers in all boxes.** Skill: Sequencing.
3	about 12 years old	Some children may answer by referring to the lion in captivity who lived until she was 25. If so, point out that this question asks when lions 'usually' live to, meaning lions in the wild. **Award 1 mark for any reference to 12 years old.** Skill: Retrieval.
4	grasslands	Some children may answer by referring to acacia trees. If so, point out that the text says the trees grow in the grasslands where the lions live. **Award 1 mark for any reference to grassland(s).** Skill: Word meaning.
5	No – because they are beautiful animals. *OR* Yes – because their numbers are declining.	Ideally, reasons will come solely from the text (e.g. references to conservation or people). However, use of some extrinsic knowledge is to be expected. **Award 1 mark for a plausible answer and justification.** Skill: Prediction.

Lions, Lions, Lions, by Laura Lodge

This is a text about the king of the beasts: the lion. It tells the reader lots of facts about how lions live.

Lions (*Panthera leo*) are the second biggest members of the 'big cat' family. Often called the kings of the beasts, they are known for their ferocious roar. Sadly, the number of lions in the world is declining and they are vulnerable to extinction.

How do lions behave?

Lions live in prides, which are groups of between 10 and 15 lions. They communicate by roaring and their roars can be heard up to 5 miles away! When a lion is born, it is called a cub. Female cubs will stay with the same pride their whole lives, but male cubs are forced to leave when they are about 2 years old. They then form their own pride of males, who look for a bigger pride to join. Lions spend most of their day sleeping – sometimes for up to 20 hours. They usually live until they are about 12 years old in the wild but a lion called Zenda lived in captivity until she was 25!

What do lions look like?

Lions are known for their sandy fur, sharp teeth and claws, and furry tufts at the ends of their tails. Males are noticeable due to their long manes, which get darker as a lion gets older. The length of an adult lion can be up to 3.5m from nose to tail and they can weigh up to 250kg!

Where do lions live?

Lions live in grasslands (or savannahs) that have acacia trees for shade. Thousands of years ago, lions lived in many parts of the world. However, they now only live in some parts of Africa and West India. Many live in protected areas such as national parks where people are working to conserve their numbers.

What do lions eat?

Lions are carnivores, which means they eat meat. They are skilled hunters and the females work together to catch medium-sized animals such as zebras, buffaloes and wildebeest. They can run up to 81km per hour, which is very helpful for catching their dinner! They are also scavengers, which means they eat animals that have already died, either from illness or by being killed by other predators. Did you know that lions need to eat up to 7kg of meat every day?

Retrieval

Name: ______________________

1 Look at the second sentence. What are lions known for?

____ 1 mark

2 Look at the section **How do lions behave?**. Why do lions roar?

____ 1 mark

3 Look at the section **What do lions look like?**. What happens to its mane as a lion gets older?

____ 1 mark

4 Look at the section **Where do lions live?**. Which parts of the world do lions live in now? Tick **two**.

Africa ☐

America ☐

India ☐

England ☐

1 mark

5 What do lions eat? Give **two** things.

____________________ and ____________________ 1 mark

Mix it up!

Name: ____________________

1 Look at the section **How do lions behave?**. How do you think the male lions feel when they are forced to leave? Why?

____

____ 2 marks

2 Male lions have a different life to female lions. Number the events to show the order in which they happen in a male lion's life. One has been done for you.

They are a cub.	1
They join up with other males.	
They look for a new pride together.	
They have to leave their pride.	

1 mark

3 Look at the section **How do lions behave?**. What age do lions usually live to?

______________________ 1 mark

4 Look at the section **Where do lions live?**. What is another word for *savannahs*?

______________________ 1 mark

5 Do you think lions will go extinct? Tick **one**.

Yes ☐ No ☐

Why?

____

____ 1 mark

There's a Lion in My Cornflakes

by Michelle Robinson

Printable text • Modelling slides   Photocopiable text and questions • pages 36 to 39

After the excitement of the real lions in Unit 1, it is now time for some fictional kings of the jungle to appear. This text is an extract from a funny story where two children try to redeem coupons for a real-life lion. This charming story is sure to engage all the children and leave them wishing for a lion in their cornflakes. After reading this text, you may wish to discuss any links or contrasts with the text in Unit 1.

1 Get ready

Discuss the **Key vocabulary** identified in the **Language toolkit** and then complete the vocabulary and phonics activities as desired. Please note that the selected vocabulary is a guide. Depending on the needs of your cohort, additional vocabulary discussion may be beneficial before, during and after reading. Next, display the text (pages 36 to 37) so the children can see the title and any illustrations, and encourage the children to discuss the following questions before reading.

1 What type of text is this? How do you know?
Fiction/a story. The children's explanations will vary but may relate to the illustration; there being no facts and figures; the idea that you can't have a lion in your cornflakes in real life.

2 We read another text about lions together. What do you think might be different in this one?
Answers will vary, though it is likely that discussion will focus on the differences between fiction and non-fiction.

3 The story is about two siblings. Have you read any other stories about brothers and sisters?
Answers will vary. You may wish to discuss the meaning of 'siblings' and whether the children have siblings.

Language toolkit

Key vocabulary

accept	apologise	ballistic
bonkers	coupon	hogging
immediate	take a fancy to	unfair

Vocabulary discussion questions

- Would it be **unfair** if you weren't allowed to got out at playtime today?
- Would you **accept** an apple instead of your usual lunch?
- What have you **taken a fancy to**?

Vocabulary activities

1 Can the children act out going **ballistic**, going **bonkers** and **hogging** something?

2 Use one of the vocabulary activities on page 15 to investigate some of the key words above.

Phonics

Decoding support words	accept, apologise, ballistic, immediate
High frequency words	Decodable: by, came, don't, made, old, time Tricky: Mr, people, their
Common exception words	bath, could, even, every, last, mind, money, Mr, old, people, poor, should, whole

Phonics activity

How many words can the children spot that include the /ai/ phoneme? The children may need support to remember the alternative graphemes for /ai/ (e.g. 'ai', 'ey', 'eigh', 'ay', 'a–e', 'ea').

2 First steps

Read the text together and then encourage the children to discuss the following questions.

1 **What happened at the very beginning of the text?**
Answers will vary but should relate to seeing the offer of a free lion for 100 coupons. Some of the children may refer to the supermarket alone. If so, encourage them to reread the first few sentences.

2 **Who are the main characters?**
Two brothers called Eric and Dan. The children may need support to find Eric's name as it comes later in the text.

3 **This is a story but there is another type of text in the middle of the story. What type of text is it?**
A letter.

4 **Did you like the text? Why? Why not?**
Answers will vary but encourage the children to explain their answers (e.g. *I liked it because it was funny when the crocodile was delivered*).

3 Explore

- Discuss with the children whether they would do the same as Eric and Dan. Would they want a pet lion? How about one of the other wild animals in the story (gorilla, crocodile, grizzly bear)? Would they eat 100 boxes of cornflakes to get one? Talk about the pros and cons of owning the animal.
- Discuss whether the children think it would be fair to the lion and the other animals in the story to live as people's pets. Encourage the children to use the knowledge they learnt in Unit 1, including your discussion about zoos.
- The author uses lots of humour in the story. Discuss how the author makes the book funny (e.g. bathroom-hogging crocodile; use of capital letters).

4 Skills focus

See pages 34 to 35

Use the information from the **Skills guide** and the relevant **Skills graphic** to introduce the skill of inference.

1 Model the skill using the **Unit 2 Modelling slides** and the **Modelling inference** guidance on page 34.

2 The children can then attempt the **Inference** questions on page 38.

3 Finally, the **Mix it up!** questions on page 39 offer practice in a range of comprehension skills.

Answers and marking guidance for all questions are included on pages 34 to 35.

5 Where next?

- Speaking and listening task: The children could research an animal of their choice and present their newly found facts to their peers.
- Writing task: Talk to the children about what animal they would like to live in their classroom. Work together to write a persuasive letter to the head teacher about getting a class pet. The children could first work in pairs to come up with their own reasons and some of these could then be incorporated into the class letter.

Reading list

Fiction
- *The Most Magnificent Thing* by Ashley Spires
- *Strictly No Elephants* by Lisa Mantchev

Class reads
- *Have You Seen My Giraffe?* by Michelle Robinson

Non-fiction
- *An Anthology of Intriguing Animals* by Ben Hoare
- *Crazy About Cats* by Owen Davey
- *Lions, Lions, Lions* by Laura Lodge
(Linked text: Unit 1)

Poetry
- *Animal Poems* by Jennifer Curry

Modelling inference

See Unit 2 Modelling slides

Use the **Skills guide** (see pages 20 to 21) and the downloadable **Skills graphic** to support your modelling.

1 Read the first two sentences. Did Eric think getting a free lion was a good idea? How do you know?

No – because he told us to ignore it.

Read the question together and model using the locator and key words to find the right part of the text. Model finding a link in the text to support your answer and encourage children to do this. Some children may attempt to use knowledge from later in the text (e.g. *No, because they get a crocodile and gorilla instead*). If so, remind them about the locator. Some children may answer 'yes' because of knowledge from the second paragraph. If so, look at the question again together and emphasise 'Read the first two sentences'.

2 Why do you think Mum was *mad* after Eric and Dan bought the cereal?

The children had wasted all their pocket money.

Read the question together and model finding the key word 'mad' in the text. Ask the children to imagine they are Eric and Dan's mum. Think aloud as you put yourself in Mum's shoes: *Why might I be feeling angry?* Discuss the likely reasons (e.g. she didn't want 100 boxes of cornflakes or a lion; the children spent all their money). Model writing a plausible answer.

3 *... everyone else had the same idea. Poor postman.* Why did Eric feel sorry for the postman?

Because he was having to deliver real lions to almost everybody.

Read the question together and model finding the locator. Point out that the text says 'everyone else'. Ask the children what that tells us. Think aloud: *Why might that be bad for the postman?* Ask the children to imagine how the postman feels – would he prefer to deliver a letter or a lion? Why? Encourage the children to discuss the difficulties of delivering lions, such as the weight or size of them, or the danger involved.

4 Look at the paragraph beginning *We waited and waited ...* . How do you think Eric and Dan felt when their lion didn't get delivered?

angry

Read the question together and model finding the locator. Point out that the text says that everyone else had got their lion except Eric and Dan. Think aloud: *How would you feel if everyone in the class had something they wanted except you?* If the children all respond with words such as 'sad', ask them to explain why and discuss other similar words, such as 'jealous', 'frustrated' and 'disappointed', to help them understand the nuance of the text. You could also point out that Eric and Dan had been promised something by the company that they have not been given.

Inference questions mark scheme

See page 38

Answer		Guidance
1	excited	Some children may focus on the cornflakes (e.g. bored with eating cornflakes). If so, refocus them on looking at the reason behind eating the cornflakes. **Award 1 mark for a plausible emotion.**
2	frustrated/angry/surprised	Some children may respond with 'excited' due to their own feelings about receiving a grizzly bear. If so, encourage them to go back to the text to look at Eric and Dan's reactions. **Award 1 mark for a plausible emotion.**
3	A crocodile is dangerous/has sharp teeth.	**Award 1 mark for any reference to crocodiles being dangerous animals. Also accept references to animals needing to be looked after.**

Answer		Guidance
4	angry ☑	Some children may choose 'tired' as they may say he was tired of the wrong animal being delivered. If so, encourage them to reread the sentence beginning "A crocodile?" and say it out loud as if they were Dan. You could point out that the punctuation suggests he felt a stronger emotion. **Award 1 mark for the correct answer ticked.**
5	The gorilla broke/destroyed Dad's car/ wouldn't leave it alone.	Some children may reason that, as 'taking a fancy to' indicates a positive feeling, the gorilla did something good. This is acceptable, as the nuance may not be clear, but it may be worth discussing the gorilla's likely actions. **Award 1 mark for any reference to the gorilla breaking Dad's car or not leaving it alone.**

Mix it up! questions mark scheme

See page 39

Answer		Guidance
1	ride it to school. ☑	The children may tick the other two options because they are relying on their extrinsic knowledge. Remind them that this is a retrieval question so we have to find the answer in the text. **Award 1 mark for the correct answer ticked.** **Skill: Retrieval.**
2	grumpy *OR* grumpy mum *OR* a grumpy mum	Some children may find this tricky at first and give longer answers. They may need this to be modelled for them. **Award 1 mark for a correct answer. Accept only the answers opposite with no additional words.** **Skill: Word meaning.**
3	gorilla [3] crocodile [2] grizzly bear [1]	Encourage the children to find, highlight and number each animal in the text before filling in the answer boxes. **Award 1 mark for the correct numbers in all boxes.** **Skill: Sequencing.**
4	annoyed/angry	Answers will vary but will probably tend towards the negative. **Award 1 mark for a plausible emotion. Accept plausible positive emotions such as 'looking forward to finally getting the lion'.** **Skill: Inference.**
5	Eric and Dan will complain to the cereal company again.	Encourage the children to verbally justify their prediction. **Award 1 mark for a plausible prediction linked to the events in the text.** **Skill: Prediction.**

There's a Lion in My Cornflakes, by Michelle Robinson

This is an extract from *There's a Lion in My Cornflakes*, a story about two brothers who collect coupons and expect to get a free lion in the post.

If you ever see this on a packet of cornflakes:

FREE LION, JUST SAVE 100 COUPONS

Ignore it! You should see what happened when we didn't ...

Me and my brother, Dan, made umpteen trips to the supermarket and spent a whole year's pocket money on cereal. It took us AGES to cut out all the coupons. Mum was so mad, she made us eat cornflakes for breakfast, lunch and tea. She said we'd have nothing but cornflakes until they were all gone. That could take forever! And she said there'd be no more pocket money until we'd eaten up every last boring, crunchy flake. But we didn't mind. We really wanted a free lion. We could take it for walks. Ride it to school. And use it to open tin cans.* Mind you, it seems everyone else had the same idea. Poor postman.

*Don't try this at home with your cat!

We waited and waited for our free lion to arrive. But there was no lion on Monday ... or Tuesday ... or Wednesday. Thursday? No lion. Friday? No lion. Saturday? STILL no lion. Even worse, by the time Sunday came ... EVERYONE else had theirs. How unfair is that?! Then on Monday, a delivery truck arrived. We were so excited! But, one: it wasn't a lion. Two: they sent it next door by mistake, and three: it went ballistic in Mr Harper's back yard. It wasn't our fault! But Mum went bonkers. She made us apologise to Mr Harper AND tidy up. It was awful. We had a grizzly bear, a grumpy mum and absolutely NO free lion. We wrote to the cereal people and complained. They wrote back:

> Dear Eric and Dan,
>
> Sorry about the grizzly bear, but we ran out of lions. Please accept this crocodile instead.
>
> Yours sincerely,
>
> Mr Flaky.
>
> P.S. Handle with care.

"A crocodile?!" Dan said. "We didn't eat all those cornflakes for a cranky old crocodile!" And guess what? The crocodile spent all its time in the bathroom, so no one else could get in. Dad went nuts. He made us scrub the bath while he telephoned the cereal people. "Sorry," they said. "We'll sort it out straight away."

We asked for a LION. NOT a grizzly bear, NOT a bathroom-hogging crocodile and ... DEFINITELY not a whacking great gorilla. But that's exactly what we got. It took an immediate fancy to Dad's car. He was not impressed.

Inference

Name: ____________________

1 Look at the paragraph beginning *Me and my brother ...* . How did Dan and Eric feel when they sent in their coupons?

______________________________ 1 mark

2 Look at the top of the second page. How did Eric and Dan feel when the grizzly bear was delivered?

______________________________ 1 mark

3 Look at the letter. Why do you think Mr Flaky told them to handle the crocodile with care?

______________________________ 1 mark

4 How did Dan feel when the crocodile was delivered? Tick **one**.

upset ☐

excited ☐

angry ☐

tired ☐

1 mark

5 Look at the paragraph beginning *We asked for ...* . What do you think the gorilla did to Dad's car?

______________________________ 1 mark

Mix it up!

Name: ____________________

1 Look at the paragraph starting *Me and my brother ...* . Why did Eric and Dan want the lion? Tick **one**.

Eric and Dan wanted the lion so they could ...

ride it in races. ☐

use it to scare burglars. ☐

ride it to school. ☐

1 mark

2 *We had a grizzly bear, a grumpy mum and absolutely NO free lion.* Find and copy **one** word that means the same as 'annoyed'.

____

1 mark

3 Number the animals to show the order in which they were sent to the children. One has been done for you.

gorilla [3]

crocodile ☐

grizzly bear ☐

1 mark

4 How did Eric and Dan feel at the end of the story?

____

1 mark

5 What do you predict will happen next in the story?

____

____

____

1 mark

The Great Fire of London

by Emma Adams

Printable text • Modelling slides Photocopiable text and questions • pages 44 to 47

The Great Fire of London is one of the most famous events in the city's history. This unit's text explains how the fire started and where it spread first. This unit is linked to Unit 4, which tells another famous tale from the same period in history – that of Guy Fawkes and the Gunpowder Plot. After completing both units, you may wish to discuss how the stories are both true, historical accounts but they are written in different ways: Unit 4's text is written as a traditional information text, while this unit's text conveys the information in the form of a narrative.

1 Get ready

Discuss the **Key vocabulary** identified in the **Language toolkit** and then complete the vocabulary and phonics activities as desired. Please note that the selected vocabulary is a guide. Depending on the needs of your cohort, additional vocabulary discussion may be beneficial before, during and after reading. Next, display the text (pages 44 to 45) so the children can see the title and any illustrations, and encourage the children to discuss the following questions before reading.

1 Have you ever heard of the Great Fire of London?
Answers will vary depending on the children's experience. If they have heard of the Great Fire, encourage them to share what they know with one another. Encourage discussion of the word 'great' – does it mean great in size or does it express a positive emotion? If the children have never heard of this event, you may need to discuss the size and scale of it. You could ask the children how they would feel if all the houses in their area were on fire.

2 What type of text is this? How do you know?
The children are likely to say that it looks like fiction or a story. Although this is correct, remind the children of your discussion of the previous question to help them to understand that the text is based on fact.

3 Can you think of any other famous events that happened in the United Kingdom a long time ago?
Answers will vary depending on the children's experience. Encourage the children to share their ideas about this even if they are unsure about them.

4 Have you ever read any other books that are set a long time ago?
Answers will vary depending on the children's exposure to texts, but they should be able to contribute examples of fiction, non-fiction or both.

Language toolkit

Key vocabulary

ashes	beaten down	combination
deny	ember	licked
rose	thatched	troubled

Vocabulary discussion questions

- Is **rose** a flower or an action? Can it be both?
- When have you been **troubled** by something?
- When I mix flour and water to make bread, am I making a **combination**?

Vocabulary activities

1 When do we use the verb **licked**? Discuss how it is normally used when discussing food but in this case it is used for the flames. Can the children think of any other verbs that can be used in different ways?

2 Use one of the vocabulary activities on page 15 to investigate some of the key words above.

Phonics

Decoding support words	**buildings, continued, mayor, southwards, Thames, throughout, warehouses**
High frequency words	Decodable: **by, day, house, made, put, time** Tricky: **asked, could, people**
Common exception words	**because, busy, could, even, great, most, move, only, people, sure, would**

Phonics activity

How many words can the children spot that include the /oo/ phoneme?

2 First steps

Read the text together and then encourage the children to discuss the following questions.

1 **Who was Thomas Farriner?**
He was the baker to King Charles II and he owned a busy bakery on Pudding Lane.

2 **When did the fire start?**
In the early hours of Sunday 2nd September 1666. Some children may respond with 'Saturday'. In this case, refocus them on the sentence beginning 'In the early hours …'.

3 **Which other people are there in the story?**
The maid; Samuel Pepys; King Charles II; Sir Thomas Bludworth, the Lord Mayor of London.

4 **Did you like the text? Why? Why not?**
Answers will vary but encourage the children to explain their answers (e.g. *I liked finding out about the fire in a story but I want to know what happened next!*).

3 Explore

- Discuss how lucky we are that we have smoke alarms now, and that buildings are built from less flammable materials than wood. Point out that even in modern times it is still very important to keep ourselves safe from fire. Discuss what we can do to keep ourselves safe and prevent fires. What should we do if we find a fire in school or at home?
- Samuel Pepys wrote a very famous diary about life in London during the 1600s. Discuss whether any of the children write their own diaries. What might we include in a diary entry written about our day today?
- The author gives information about the Great Fire of London but she has written the facts like a story. To help illustrate this, you could draw the children's attention to phrases like 'some say' and 'others say', as well as to instances of emotive language and personification (e.g. 'sprang back to life', 'dying fire', 'the fire … licked', 'deadly'). Can a fire really lick or die? Discuss why the author might have written in this style rather than in the more traditional non-fiction style of Units 1 and 4. Which do the children prefer, and why?

4 Skills focus

See pages 42 to 43

Use the information from the **Skills guide** and the relevant **Skills graphic** to introduce the skill of retrieval.

1 Model the skill using the **Unit 3 Modelling slides** and the **Modelling retrieval** guidance on page 42.

2 The children can then attempt the **Retrieval** questions on page 46.

3 Finally, the **Mix it up!** questions on page 47 offer practice in a range of comprehension skills.

Answers and marking guidance for all questions are included on pages 42 to 43.

5 Where next?

- Speaking and listening task: The children could research what happened next during the Great Fire of London by reading extracts from Samuel Pepys' diary (see **Reading list**). They could work in small groups to retell the story in their own words to another class or year group.
- Writing task: Following on from your class discussion during **Explore**, the children could create fire safety posters to display around school. These could include tips on how to prevent fires as well as what to do if you ever encounter one.

Reading list

Fiction

- *The Baker's Boy and the Great Fire of London* by Tom Bradman and Tony Bradman

Class reads

- *Raven Boy* by Pippa Goodhart

Non-fiction

- *Great Fire of London Activity Book* by Sally Jane Morgan
- *Guy Fawkes* by Laura Lodge (Linked text: Unit 4)
- *Samuel Pepys* by Izzi Howell
- *See Inside London* by Rob Lloyd Jones
- *Who was: Samuel Pepys?* by Paul Harrison
- *You Wouldn't Want to Be in the Great Fire of London!* by Jim Pipe

Poetry

- 'The Great Fire of London' by Paul Perro

Websites

- The National Archives website offers a free 'Great Fire of London game'.

Modelling retrieval

See Unit 3 Modelling slides

Use the **Skills guide** (see pages 16 to 17) and the downloadable **Skills graphic** to support your modelling.

1 Look at the first paragraph. What was lit every day in the bakery? Tick <u>one</u>.

the fire ☐ the stone ☐ the oven ☑ the bread ☐

Read the question together and remind the children that this is a retrieval question. Model identifying the key words. The distractors (incorrect answers) in this question could prove challenging for some children as they all occur in the text. Think aloud: *We need to use the key words from the question.* Model using the locator to find the relevant part of the text, and scanning for the sentence beginning 'The large stone oven …'. You could use 'Fastest finger first' (see page 17) to demonstrate that you have used the text to answer the question.

2 Look at the second paragraph. Give <u>one</u> reason why the fire might have started.

An ember fell from the oven and set fire to some wood. *OR* They had forgotten to sweep out the oven so the fire sprang back to life.

Read the question together and model using the locator and key word 'started' to find the right part of the text. Continue by reading the paragraph and discuss the reasons given for the fire starting. Encourage the children to prove their responses by using 'Fastest finger first'. Some children may choose to answer vaguely from memory (e.g. the fire was not completely out). If so, remind them that we are retrieving information and therefore we must take our response from the text.

3 Look at the third paragraph. From how far away could the fire be seen?

from a quarter of a mile away

Read the question together and model using the locator and key words (e.g. from how far away, seen) to find the relevant information. Think aloud: *Which words tell me how far away the fire could be seen?* You may wish to check children's understanding by modelling writing a vague response, such as 'quarter', and asking them whether the answer is specific enough. Discuss the need to include 'from a quarter of a mile away' to answer the question properly.

4 Draw lines to show what each person did during the fire

Pepys	created a firebreak
Thomas Farriner	asked the King to take action
The Lord Mayor of London	owned bakery where fire started

Read the question together. It is likely that the children will have had few opportunities to attempt matching questions, therefore it is particularly important to spend time discussing the type of question this is and modelling how to approach it. This question requires the children to understand the whole text, therefore it is important to spend additional time identifying the key words to support finding the information. Model identifying the key words 'Pepys', 'Mayor' and 'Farriner', and scanning the text for them one at a time, discussing each against the three options. Make sure to model matching each person and action.

Retrieval questions mark scheme

See page 46

Answer	Guidance
1 Pudding Lane	Some children may use the question stem and respond with 'east London'. In this case, reread the question together and explain that we cannot use words that are in the question itself. **Award 1 mark for the correct answer.**
2 Thomas Farriner ☑ the maid ☑	If the children rely on their memory of the text and respond incorrectly, refocus them on the locator and the key word 'blamed'. **Award 2 marks for the correct answers ticked.**

Answer		Guidance
3	the wind	Some children may use inference skills and answer 'dry wooden frames', or use extrinsic knowledge about the fire. These answers should not be accepted. In this case, refocus the children by supporting them to scan for the key word 'helped' within the paragraph. Remind them that the answer will be very close to this word. **Award 1 mark for any reference to the wind.**
4	houses	Some children may benefit from being provided with a locator or being encouraged to scan for the word 'firebreak' to help answer this question. **Award 1 mark for any reference to houses or buildings.**
5	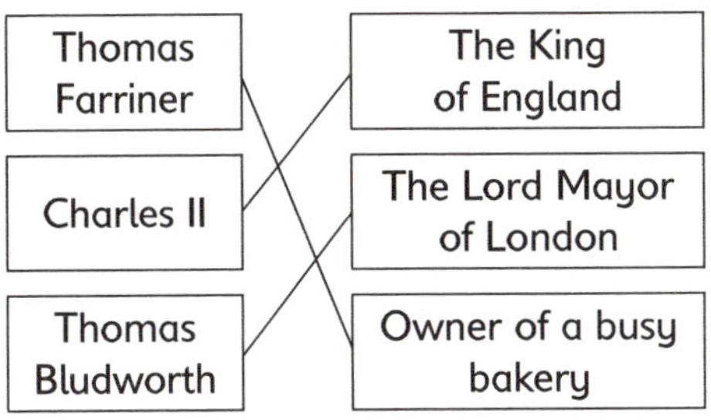	This question requires that the children understand the whole text. As it may be the first time the children are attempting a matching question independently, you may wish to provide two statements already matched up (e.g. 'Thomas Farriner' matched to 'owner of a busy bakery'). **Award 1 mark for all pairs correctly matched.**

Mix it up! questions mark scheme

See page 47

Answer		Guidance
1	flames	If the children respond with more than one word, remind them of the rules of 'find and copy' questions and model this again if necessary. Some children may respond using the word 'ashes'. In this case, you may need to explain the difference between a fire and its ashes. **Award 1 mark for the correct answer. Also accept 'flame' or 'the flames' as the children may not yet be confident with this question type.** Skill: Word meaning.
2	the maid	If the children find this question challenging, remind them to identify a key word ('killed') and scan the paragraph for that word before reading around it. **Award 1 mark for the correct answer.** Skill: Retrieval.
3	upset ✓	Children with strong inference skills may argue that these people were happy that the fire would be put out, or that they felt a mixture of emotions. In this case, discuss the clues in the text ('most people didn't want …') and then ask them to choose the most appropriate option from those listed. **Award 1 mark for the correct answer ticked.** Skill: Inference.
4	the Mayor ✓	Encourage the children to find, highlight and number each of the possible answers in the text before filling in the answer boxes. **Award 1 mark for the correct answer ticked.** Skill: Sequencing.
5	It might rain./People will bring water./ Firefighters might come.	This is a tricky prediction question as it is not obvious that it is asking for a prediction. The children may use extrinsic knowledge, which should be accepted. **Award 1 mark for a plausible prediction.** Skill: Prediction.

The Great Fire of London, by Emma Adams

This text is from a longer story which tells the true story of the Great Fire of London in 1666. This text tells us about when the fire started in a bakery on Pudding Lane.

Thomas Farriner owned a busy bakery on Pudding Lane, in east London. He was the baker to Charles II, the king at that time. The large stone oven in the bakery was lit in the early hours of each morning and burned throughout the day. At night, as the bakery was closing, the flames were beaten down to ashes. But on Saturday 1st September 1666, no one made sure that the fire in Farriner's bakery had been properly put out. The oven continued to burn, and no one noticed ...

In the early hours of Sunday morning, the Great Fire of London started. Some say it was because a hot ember fell from the oven and set fire to a nearby pile of wood. Others say that Farriner had forgotten to sweep out the oven, which meant that the dying fire sprang back to life. Even Farriner's maid was blamed – although she never had the chance to deny this, because she was one of the first people to be killed by the fire.

By 3 o'clock in the morning, flames rose high above Pudding Lane and could be seen from a quarter of a mile away. A strong wind helped the fire move quickly, blowing it west from house to house. It fed off the dry wooden frames of buildings and licked at thatched roofs and pitch, pushing southwards towards London Bridge. If the fire travelled across the bridge, everyone and everything south of the river would also be in great danger.

The only way to stop the fire from spreading was to create a firebreak – houses had to be pulled down to create space between the fire and the buildings still standing. Most people didn't want to tear down their homes, but nothing else would stop the fire. Pepys went to King Charles and asked him to take action. The King was deeply troubled by Pepys' visit and sent him to deliver his message to the Lord Mayor of London, Sir Thomas Bludworth. The Mayor was sent into a panic, shouting, "Lord! What can I do? ... I have been pulling down houses, but the fire overtakes us faster than we can do it." The fire continued to spread west towards Thames Street, to warehouses filled with oil and alcohol. This deadly combination fed the flames and made the fire even more dangerous.

Retrieval

Name: ______________________________

1 Where in east London was Thomas Farriner's bakery?

______________________________ 1 mark

2 Look at the second paragraph. Who was blamed for the fire starting? Tick **two**.

the King ☐

Thomas Farriner ☐

the maid ☐

the Mayor ☐

2 marks

3 Look at the third paragraph. What helped the fire?

______________________________ 1 mark

4 What was pulled down to make a firebreak?

______________________________ 1 mark

5 Draw lines to match the person to the job they had in the story.

Thomas Farriner	The King of England
Charles II	The Lord Mayor of London
Thomas Bludworth	Owner of a busy bakery

1 mark

Mix it up!

Name: ______________________________

1 *At night, as the bakery was closing, the flames were beaten down to ashes.* Find and copy **one** word that means the same as 'fire'.

____

1 mark

2 Look at the second paragraph. Who was one of the people killed by the fire?

____

1 mark

3 Look at the last paragraph. How do you think the people felt when their houses were pulled down? Tick **one**.

upset ☐

bored ☐

happy ☐

excited ☐

1 mark

4 Look at the last paragraph. Who did Pepys speak to last? Tick **one**.

his wife ☐

the King ☐

Farriner ☐

the Mayor ☐

1 mark

5 What do you think will help stop the fire?

____

____

____

1 mark

Guy Fawkes

by Laura Lodge

Printable text • Modelling slides   Photocopiable text and questions • pages 52 to 55

Children all over the United Kingdom will be familiar with Bonfire Night on 5th November. To many, the celebration will be about fireworks, but do they know the story behind it? This text, a child-friendly biography of Guy Fawkes, explains why we celebrate Bonfire Night. You could make comparisons between this unit and Unit 3, which covers the Great Fire of London, as both use non-fiction texts based on historical events.

1 Get ready

Discuss the **Key vocabulary** identified in the **Language toolkit** and then complete the vocabulary and phonics activities as desired. Please note that the selected vocabulary is a guide. Depending on the needs of your cohort, additional vocabulary discussion may be beneficial before, during and after reading. Next, display the text (pages 52 to 53) so the children can see the title and any illustrations, and encourage the children to discuss the following questions before reading.

1. What type of text is this? How do you know?
   Most of the children will probably assume it is fictional unless they already know about this episode in history. If so, point out the factual information and dates in the text.
2. Do you know who Guy Fawkes is?
   Answers will vary. Some children may have no knowledge of him but others may know he's connected to Bonfire Night.
3. Have you been to a bonfire or seen a fireworks display before? Did you enjoy it?
   Answers will vary. If some children have not experienced one or either, show photos or video clips to support discussion.
4. Do you know why we have bonfires and fireworks on the 5th November every year?
   Answers will vary depending on the children's extrinsic knowledge and experiences.

Language toolkit

Key vocabulary

disagreements	execute	fuses
gunpowder	Houses of Parliament	monarch
plotting	raise the alarm	worshipping

Vocabulary discussion questions

- When did you last have a **disagreement**?
- Is Queen Elizabeth II our **monarch**?
- Who works at the **Houses of Parliament**?

Vocabulary activities

1. Ask the children how many synonyms they can find that mean something similar to **disagreement**.
2. Use one of the vocabulary activities on page 15 to investigate some of the key words above.

Phonics

Decoding support words	Catholic, monarch, Parliament, Protestant, worshipping
High frequency words	Decodable: about, by, day, houses, made, time, very Tricky: called, could, people
Common exception words	because, could, even, every, past, people, should, told, would

Phonics activity

How many words can the children spot that include the /ch/ phoneme? The children may need support to remember the alternative graphemes for /ch/ (e.g. 'ture', 'ch', 'tch').

2 First steps

Read the text together and then encourage the children to discuss the following questions.

1 **When did Guy Fawkes live?**
Answers will vary from exact (e.g. *1570–1606*) to vague (e.g. *a long time ago/the past/Tudor times*).

2 **Why is he still important in the United Kingdom?**
He is important because he's the reason we celebrate Bonfire Night.

3 **What happened to Guy at the end of the text?**
He was executed./He died. Some children may say he was burned on a bonfire (confusing Guy with a guy) – reread the relevant part together if needed and link to knowledge of proper nouns.

4 **Did you like the text? Why? Why not?**
Answers will vary but encourage the children to explain their answers (e.g. *I liked it because it had lots of facts that I didn't know before*).

3 Explore

- Compare this text with the non-fiction texts in Units 1 and 3. What is similar and what is different about them? Which do the children think is the most useful way of presenting the information? Could we improve this text by including other features (e.g. timeline, subheadings)?
- Discuss the children's opinion of Guy Fawkes. Do they think he did the right thing? Have the children ever had to stand up for themselves or for someone else? Explore the idea that he was right to stand up for his beliefs but that he did not choose a peaceful way to do this.

4 Skills focus

See pages 50 to 51

Use the information from the **Skills guide** and the relevant **Skills graphic** to introduce the skill of retrieval.

1 Model the skill using the **Unit 4 Modelling slides** and the **Modelling retrieval** guidance on page 50.

2 The children can then attempt the **Retrieval** questions on page 54.

3 Finally, the **Mix it up!** questions on page 55 offer practice in a range of comprehension skills.

Answers and marking guidance for all questions are included on pages 50 to 51.

5 Where next?

- Speaking and listening task: Encourage the children to explore the emotions of Guy Fawkes and King James through a 'hot seat' activity. In this activity, a child plays a character and is interviewed by the rest of the class or group. The children could take turns to sit in the 'hot seat' and answer questions as if they were Guy Fawkes or King James. Questions to Guy Fawkes might be: *Why were you angry at the King? Why did you decide to blow up the Houses of Parliament?* Questions to King James might be: *How did you feel when you found out about the Gunpowder Plot? Why do you think it's important to celebrate on 5th November?*
- Writing task: The children could write a letter as Guy Fawkes explaining why he has decided to blow up the King. Who would he write a letter to? What would he say to explain his actions? How does he feel about what he has decided to do?

Reading list

Fiction

- *The Gunpowder Plot* by Rob Lloyd Jones

Class reads

- *You Wouldn't Want to Be Guy Fawkes!* by Fiona Macdonald

Non-fiction

- *Bonfire Night* by Nancy Dickmann
- *The Great Fire of London* by Emma Adams (Linked text: Unit 3)
- *Why Do We Remember? Guy Fawkes and the Gunpowder* Plot by Izzi Howell

Poetry

- *Let's Celebrate! Festival Poems from Around the World* by Debjani Chatterjee and Brian D'Arcy

Plays

- *The Gunpowder Plot (Putting on a Play)* by Tony Bradman and Tom Bradman

Modelling retrieval

See Unit 4 Modelling slides

Use the **Skills guide** (see pages 16 to 17) and the downloadable **Skills graphic** to support your modelling.

1 **Look at the paragraph beginning *Guy, or Guido …* . Where was Guy Fawkes born?**

York

Read the question together and model using the locator and key words (e.g. 'born') to support finding the information. Some children may respond with 'England'. If so, model checking to see if there is anything more specific in the text. Model and encourage the children to use 'Fastest finger first' (see page 17) to prove the answer is in the text.

2 **Look at the paragraph beginning *In 1593 …* . What did Guy do when he was 23?**

He became a soldier in the Spanish army and fought for the Catholic Church.

Read the question together and model using the locator and key words (e.g. 'Guy', '23') and scanning the text for them. Discuss with the children the things Guy did when he was 23 (e.g. *he was a soldier; he was a Spanish soldier; he was a soldier and fought for the Catholic Church*). Discuss which response is best and ask the children to explain why. Model writing the answer with the children's input.

3 **Look at the paragraph beginning *In 1593 …* . Who led the group that was plotting to blow up the King?**

Robert Catesby

Read the question together and model using the locator to find the relevant part of the text. Model identifying the key word 'plotting' and scanning the text for it. Think aloud: *Who can find the word the fastest?* Some children may assume the answer is Guy Fawkes. If so, discuss what this paragraph tells us, in order to explain why the answer cannot be Guy. Reread the paragraph together to find the correct answer.

4 **Look at the paragraph beginning *In March 1605 …* . How did the soldiers know where to find Guy?**

A letter was sent to Lord Monteagle.

Read the question together and model using the locator to find the right part of the text. Model identifying the key word 'soldiers' and scanning the text for it. Discuss how the soldiers knew where to find Guy and explore the children's responses (e.g. *a letter* [insufficient detail]; *Lord Monteagle was sent a letter; Lord Monteagle was sent a letter and he told the King*). Discuss which response is best and ask the children to explain why. Model writing the answer with the children's input.

Retrieval questions mark scheme

See page 54

Answer	Guidance
1 Guido	Some children may need to discuss what 'known by' means prior to attempting this question. **Award 1 mark for the correct answer and accept any misspellings.**
2 in charge of the Church	Some children may confuse Henry VIII with the Pope. If so, reread the second paragraph together. **Award 1 mark for the correct answer.**
3 36/thirty-six	Some children may respond with other numbers from the text (e.g. '23', '1605', '26'). Model scanning the text for 'barrels' to ensure they find the correct answer quickly. **Award 1 mark for the correct answer.**

Answer	Guidance
4 Lord Monteagle ☑	Some children may choose 'King James' as he was the one who ordered the soldiers to arrest Guy. If this misconception occurs, reread the corresponding paragraph together. **Award 1 mark for the correct answer ticked.**
5 to celebrate the Gunpowder Plot being stopped	Some children may respond with 'to celebrate Guy Fawkes' or similar. If so, clarify that it's celebrating his death and the end of the plot, not celebrating him. **Award 1 mark for any reference to celebrating the Gunpowder Plot being stopped.**

Mix it up! questions mark scheme

See page 55

Answer	Guidance
1 captured	If the children find this tricky, you may wish to spend some time discussing the meaning of 'caught' and possible synonyms. **Award 1 mark for the correct answer. Also accept 'was captured', but no other additional words.** **Skill: Word meaning.**
2 Guy joined the army. [2] Guy joined the plotters. [3] Guy was born in York. [1] Guy died. [5] Guy was arrested. [4]	The events take place over several paragraphs, so encourage the children to look at the whole text, thinking about what happens at the beginning, middle and end of the story. If the children find this challenging, you could ask them to find, highlight and number the events in the text before filling in the answer boxes. **Award 1 mark for the correct numbers in at least 2 boxes and 2 marks for the correct numbers in all boxes.** **Skill: Sequencing.**
3 scared/upset	Ask the children to verbally explain their opinions to check their understanding (e.g. *He was upset because his plan hadn't worked*). **Award 1 mark for any reference to a plausible emotion.** **Skill: Inference.**
4 1606	Some children may respond with other dates from the text (e.g. '1605'). Encourage them to reread the penultimate paragraph and scan for a date. **Award 1 mark for the correct answer.** **Skill: Retrieval.**
5 Yes – to celebrate the Gunpowder Plot being stopped. *OR* No – because it celebrates someone's death.	Some children may respond with explanations that use extrinsic knowledge (e.g. 'Yes, because fireworks are beautiful'). If so, accept these answers if the explanation is linked to the text. **Award 1 mark for a plausible prediction.** **Skill: Prediction.**

Guy Fawkes, by Laura Lodge

This text tells us all about the life of the man who inspired Bonfire Night.

Have you ever been to a bonfire or seen a fireworks display on Bonfire Night on 5th November? Did you know that you are actually celebrating the day that a man called Guy Fawkes was captured?

Guy, or Guido, Fawkes was born in York on 13th April 1570. In England at that time, there were lots of disagreements about what religion people should be. In the past, all English people were Catholic, which meant that they believed that the Pope was in charge of the Church. In 1532, King Henry VIII decided he wanted to be in charge of the Church instead because he disagreed with the Pope. From this time, everyone in England was told to be Protestant instead and follow the Church of England, led by the King or Queen. Some people did not want to change their religion and so they continued to be Catholic, often worshipping in secret as they could be punished if the monarch found out. Even though Guy Fawkes' family were all Protestant, he decided to become a Catholic.

In 1593, when he was 23, he even became a soldier in the Spanish army and fought for the Catholic Church. In 1603, James I was crowned King and things became even more dangerous for Catholics. King James' behaviour made Guy Fawkes very angry, so in 1604 he decided to return to England and join a group plotting to get rid of

him. The group, led by Robert Catesby, decided to blow up the King when he was at the opening of the Houses of Parliament.

In March 1605, the plotters hid 36 barrels of gunpowder in the cellars underneath the Houses of Parliament. Everything was going to plan and Guy thought that England would get rid of King James for good. However, there was a spy in the group. On 26th October 1605, a secret letter was sent to Lord Monteagle, warning him not to go to the Houses of Parliament on 5th November. Lord Monteagle raised the alarm and a trap was set for the plotters. On the morning of 5th November 1605, soldiers arrested Guy Fawkes just as he was about to light the fuses.

All of the members of the Gunpowder Plot were arrested and taken to the Tower of London. On 31st January 1606 Guy Fawkes and his group were executed.

King James decided that 5th November should always be celebrated as the day the Gunpowder Plot was stopped. Since then, people in England have celebrated every year, lighting bonfires and setting off fireworks. Some people even burn 'guys' – dolls that are meant to look like Guy Fawkes.

Retrieval

Name: ____________________

1 Look at the second paragraph. What name was Guy Fawkes also known by?

____

1 mark

2 Look at the second paragraph. What did Henry VIII want to be?

____

1 mark

3 How many barrels of gunpowder were hidden in the cellars?

____

1 mark

4 Look at the fourth paragraph. Who was sent a letter warning him about the plot? Tick **one**.

Guy Fawkes ☐

Robert Catesby ☐

King James ☐

Lord Monteagle ☐

1 mark

5 Why do some people burn dolls known as 'guys' on Bonfire Night?

____

____

1 mark

Mix it up!

Name: ______________________

1 *Did you know that you are actually celebrating the day that a man called Guy Fawkes was captured?*
Find and copy **one** word that means the same as 'caught'.

______________________ 1 mark

2 Number the events to show the order in which they happened in the text. One has been done for you.

Guy joined the army. ☐

Guy joined the plotters. ☐

Guy was born in York. 1

Guy died. ☐

Guy was arrested. ☐

2 marks

3 How do you think Guy Fawkes felt when he was arrested?

______________________ 1 mark

4 Look at the second page. In what year did Guy Fawkes die?

______________________ 1 mark

5 Do you think we will always celebrate Bonfire Night? Tick **one**.

Yes ☐ No ☐

Why?

____

____

______________________ 1 mark

Eight Candles Burning

by Celia Warren

Printable text • Modelling slides   Photocopiable text and questions • pages 60 to 63

Each year, during late November and December, Jewish families celebrate the festival of Hanukkah together. As part of their eight-night-long celebrations, candles on a menorah are lit and gifts exchanged. This poem celebrates the lighting of the candles and is a great way to encourage children to think about religions and festivals that happen during winter.

1 Get ready

Discuss the **Key vocabulary** identified in the **Language toolkit** and then complete the vocabulary and phonics activities as desired. Please note that the selected vocabulary is a guide. Depending on the needs of your cohort, additional vocabulary discussion may be beneficial before, during and after reading. Next, display the text (pages 60 to 61) so the children can see the title and any illustrations, and encourage the children to discuss the following questions before reading.

1. What type of text is this? How do you know?
   The children should be able to ascertain that it is poetry mainly due to its appearance (e.g. short lines). They should be able to talk about some basic features of poems (e.g. it *rhymes; it is organised into verses*). However, additional features may need exploring with the children.
2. Have you heard of Hanukkah before?
   Answers will vary. If you have any Jewish children in your class, take the opportunity to ask them to explain the festival. Use the illustration to explain what a menorah is and its role in the celebration. Point out that there are eight candles with a taller candle in the centre. Discuss how on each night of Hanukkah one more candle is lit until all eight are alight on the final night. The tall candle is lit every night.
3. Do you have candles burning at home sometimes?
   Answers will vary depending on the children's extrinsic knowledge. If possible, safely light a candle to show the children and explain that they were used to light houses before electricity.
4. Have you ever read any other poems or books about festivals?
   Answers will vary. Encourage the children to make links to the festivals they celebrate (e.g. Christmas, Diwali, Mawlid, Chinese New Year).

Language toolkit

Key vocabulary

alight	eager	freedom
matches	menorah	polished
promises	retold	thankful

Vocabulary discussion questions

- A candlestick can be **polished**. Can a person?
- What do you do when you set a candle **alight**?
- When was the last time you made a **promise**?

Vocabulary activities

1. The root word of **freedom** is 'free'. How many other words can the children find that begin with 'free'?
2. *The boy was* ***eager*** *to open his presents.* How many synonyms can the children find for **eager**?
3. Use one of the vocabulary activities on page 15 to investigate some of the key words above.

Phonics

Decoding support words	eager, menorah, promises
Common exception words	every, eyes, parents

Phonics activity

Ask the children to correct the sentence below.

The kandel was alite and berning.

In pairs, the children should be able to use their existing phonic knowledge to correct the spellings of 'candle', 'alight' and 'burning'.

2 First steps

Read the text together and then encourage the children to discuss the following questions.

1 **What is the poem about?**
The lighting of candles at Hanukkah. The children may only refer to the candles so it is important to link the background knowledge about Hanukkah with the candles burning in the poem.

2 **How often is a candle lit?**
Every night. The children may quote line six.

3 **Why do you think the poem is called 'Eight Candles Burning'?**
Answers will vary but should relate to the fact that eight candles are being lit on the menorah to celebrate Hanukkah.

4 **Did you like the text? Why? Why not?**
Answers will vary but encourage the children to explain their answers (e.g. *I liked it because it made me imagine lighting the candles*).

3 Explore

- Look at the poem's features together. This may be the first time the children have seen a poem like this. For example, ask the children if they can identify the key features (e.g. line and verse). You may need to teach them what these features are. Discuss the rhyming words (every verse includes 'alight' and 'night'). Draw the children's attention to any patterns (every verse ends with 'until we see eight candles burning'). Why do they think the poet has repeated the same lines at the end of every verse? Can the children find any emotive language (e.g. 'bright as the stars'; 'thankful for freedom')?
- Support the children to use the books in the **Reading list** and other materials to find out more about Hanukkah. They could also research other festivals that are celebrated in winter, paying attention to the importance of light (e.g. candles, fireworks) in the celebration of these festivals.

4 Skills focus

See pages 58 to 59

Use the information from the **Skills guide** and the relevant **Skills graphic** to introduce the skill of word meaning.

1 Model the skill using the **Unit 5 Modelling slides** and the **Modelling word meaning** guidance on page 58.

2 The children can then attempt the **Word meaning** questions on page 62.

3 Finally, the **Mix it up!** questions on page 63 offer practice in a range of comprehension skills.

Answers and marking guidance for all questions are included on pages 58 to 59.

5 Where next?

- Speaking and listening task: Discuss the different festivals the children celebrate during the year and create a class festivals calendar. Display this in the classroom and ensure that you celebrate them all together.
- Writing task: The children could use their research from **Explore** to create their own book for the school library. They could use the book to teach another year group all about Hanukkah or another winter festival of their choosing.

Reading list

Fiction

- *A Hat for Mrs Goldman* by Michelle Edwards
- *Meet the Latkes* by Alan Silberberg
- *Zigazak! A Magical Hanukkah Night* by Eric A. Kimmel

Class reads

- *The Story of Hanukkah* by David A. Adler

Non-fiction

- *Holidays Around the World: Celebrate Hanukkah* by Deborah Heiligman

Poetry

- 'Christmas Eve' by Brian Moses, from *Poems About Festivals* by Brian Moses and Kristina Swarner (Linked text: Unit 6)

Films

- *What is Hanukkah?* (CBBC *Newsround*, 2018)

Modelling word meaning

See Unit 5 Modelling slides

Use the **Skills guide** (see pages 14 to 15) and the downloadable **Skills graphic** to support your modelling.

1 Look at the first verse. Find and copy one word that means the same as 'on fire'.

burning *OR* alight

Read the question together and model using the locator. Model identifying the key words ('find and copy', 'same', 'on fire'). Think aloud: *What do we need to do to answer this question?* Explain that this 'find and copy' question asks them to copy only **one** word. If the children come up with one of the answers, see if they can locate the other word too. Explain that both words are correct but that the children must show they understand the question by choosing only one word as their answer.

2 *Parents, grandparents are children again …* What does the poet mean when she calls the adults *children*?

The poet means that they are just as excited as children are before/at a special time of year.

Read the question together and model using the locator and key words to support finding the information. Discuss with the children the differences between adults and children. Think aloud: *Why might an adult become like a child at a special time?* You could use the example of the children's feelings on Christmas Eve or the day before their birthday to support their understanding, if needed.

3 Look at the second verse. The poet says they were *thankful*. Tick one word that means the same as *thankful*.

unhappy ☐
excited ☐
grateful ☑
angry ☐

Read the question together and model finding the word 'thankful' in the verse and reading around it. The children may not be sure of the meaning of 'grateful' – this is a good opportunity to teach them the strategy of removing the incorrect choices first. Think aloud: *Do we think the answer could be 'unhappy'? Would you be unhappy/angry because you were free?* Model ticking the word 'grateful'.

4 Look at the final verse. The poet says *hearts are burning*. What does *burning* mean in this line?

It means that they are very excited and can't wait.

Read the question together and model finding the words 'hearts are burning' in the verse and reading around them. Discuss 'hearts are burning' carefully with the children. Think aloud: *Does it mean that their hearts are on fire? Or does it mean a feeling? When have you felt your hearts burning?* You could continue by referring to the word 'heart-warming' here and explaining its meaning to support the children's understanding. Be sure to check that the children do not confuse the medical condition heartburn with a heart burning.

Word meaning questions mark scheme

See page 62

	Answer	Guidance
1	two times ☑	Some children may choose three as that is how many stars are counted, or eight as this is heavily repeated in the text. If the children are not already aware that 'twice' means the same as 'two times', this should be explained clearly. **Award 1 mark for the correct answer ticked.**
2	shiny. ☑	Some children may need additional support with the meaning of 'polished'. **Award 1 mark for the correct answer ticked.**

Answer	Guidance
3 glowing/shiny/glistening	The children may need support to use the locator and to understand the word 'replace'. You could explain that this question is similar to other word meaning questions they have already encountered where they are asked to find a word that means 'the same as' another word. **Award 1 mark for a plausible adjective.**
4 happy	The children may need support to use the locator. **Award 1 mark for the correct answer.**
5 they are excited ✓	Some children may respond with 'they are hot', which shows a lack of understanding of the meaning of 'glowing' in this context. If they find this challenging, encourage them to reread the verse and help them make the connection between 'glowing' and 'stories'. Think aloud: *What is glowing and why?* **Award 1 mark for the correct answer ticked.**

Mix it up! questions mark scheme

See page 63

Answer	Guidance
1 They count the stars twice.	Some children may answer that the menorah is polished. If so, refocus them on the key word 'children' to find what the children have to do. **Award 1 mark for the correct answer. Accept 'count the stars' but do not accept 'count' on its own.** Skill: Sequencing.
2 lighting/burning a candle	The children will have encountered the word 'alight' during the discussion of the **Language toolkit** vocabulary. **Award 1 mark for any reference to lighting a candle. Do not accept minimal answers that only mention the candle or something being lit.** Skill: Word meaning.
3 matches	Some children may respond with 'menorah' – this should be clarified if needed. **Award 1 mark for the correct answer.** Skill: Retrieval.
4 excited ✓ happy ✓	Ask the children to verbally explain their opinions to check understanding (e.g. *they would be happy because they've been waiting a long time*). **Award 1 mark for the correct answers ticked.** Skill: Inference.
5 They will eat food.	The children are likely to use their extrinsic knowledge to answer. However, the prediction should link with festivals (e.g. giving gifts). **Award 1 mark for a plausible prediction.** Skill: Prediction.

Eight Candles Burning, by Celia Warren

'Eight Candles Burning' is a poem all about celebrating the Jewish festival of Hanukkah, which lasts for eight days and is also known as the 'festival of lights'.

Three stars are in the sky:
the children have counted them twice.
The menorah is polished,
the matches to hand,
ready to set a candle alight,
today, tomorrow, and every night
until we see
eight candles burning.

Bright as the stars,
the children's eyes and promises.
Parents, grandparents are children again,
thankful for freedom,
happy to set a candle alight,
today, tomorrow and every night
until we see
eight candles burning.

Around the table
faces are glowing at stories retold.
Like the flame of a match
hearts are burning,
eager to set a candle alight,
today, tomorrow and every night
until we see
eight candles burning.

Word meaning

Name: ____________________

1 How many times do the children count the stars? Tick **one**.

one time ☐

eight times ☐

three times ☐

two times ☐

1 mark

2 In the first verse the menorah is *polished*. What will it be now? Tick **one**.

It will now be ...

dull. ☐

shiny. ☐

painted. ☐

dark. ☐

1 mark

3 Look at the line *Bright as the stars*. What word could replace *bright* in this line?

____

1 mark

4 Look at the line *happy to set a candle alight*. Find and copy **one** word that means the same as 'pleased'.

____

1 mark

5 Look at the line *faces are glowing at stories retold*. What does the word *glowing* mean in this line? Tick **one**.

they are hot ☐

they are excited ☐

1 mark

Mix it up!

Name: ____________________

1 What do the children do before the candle is lit?

____ 1 mark

2 Look at the first verse. What does *set a candle alight* mean?

____ 1 mark

3 Look at the first verse. What is used to light the candle?

____________________ 1 mark

4 How do you think the people feel when all eight candles are burning?
Tick **two**.

worried ☐

excited ☐

happy ☐

warm ☐

1 mark

5 What do you think the people will do once all eight candles are lit?

____

____

____ 1 mark

Christmas Eve

by Brian Moses

Printable text • Modelling slides   Photocopiable text and questions • pages 68 to 71

Most children in the United Kingdom will be familiar with the concept of Christmas even if they do not personally celebrate it. This wonderful poem evokes the excitement and glee of children on Christmas Eve, as they eagerly wait for Father Christmas to visit. The text in Unit 5, a poem about Hanukkah, follows a similar theme and the children should be able to make links between the two poems.

1 Get ready

Discuss the **Key vocabulary** identified in the **Language toolkit** and then complete the vocabulary and phonics activities as desired. Please note that the selected vocabulary is a guide. Depending on the needs of your cohort, additional vocabulary discussion may be beneficial before, during and after reading. Next, display the text (pages 68 to 69) so the children can see the title and any illustrations, and encourage the children to discuss the following questions before reading.

1 **What type of text is this? How do you know?**
The children should easily be able to recognise this as a poem and explain its features, such as rhyming words. (See also Unit 5, **Get ready**.)

2 **Who celebrates Christmas? What happens at Christmas?**
Answers will vary depending on the children's extrinsic knowledge, but almost all the children should be able to give some response.

3 **What other festivals do people celebrate in winter?**
Answers will vary but the link to Hanukkah from Unit 5 should be easily elicited.

4 **Have you ever been really excited for something to happen? What? Why? How did you feel beforehand?**
Answers will vary depending on the children's extrinsic knowledge. Encourage them to not only talk about Christmas but share lots of exciting experiences and the build-up to them.

Language toolkit

Key vocabulary

fed up with	going round in my mind	heavenly
keep quiet	mistake	riot
settle down	terrible	wide open

Vocabulary discussion questions

- When do we **settle down** at school?
- Is a **riot** quiet?
- When were you last **fed up with** something?
- Is **terrible** the opposite of **heavenly**?

Vocabulary activities

1 Ask the children how many synonyms they can think of for **terrible**. Can they order them from strongest to weakest?

2 Use one of the vocabulary activities on page 15 to investigate some of the key words above.

Phonics

Plural –s	eyes, keeps, pies, presents, rolls
–ing suffix	baking, counting, doing, going, keeping, making, rolling, thinking, trying
Common exception words	any, Christmas, eyes, father, find, mind, pass

Phonics activity

Can the children see the pattern most of the words ending '–ing' follow (root word + 'ing')? What is different about **baking** and **making**? (The 'e' has been removed from the root words before '–ing' has been added.)

2 First steps

Read the text together and then encourage the children to discuss the following questions.

1 **What is the poem about?**
A child's feeling of excitement on Christmas Eve.

2 **Why can't the poet sleep?**
Because their mind is racing/they are so excited/they can't stop thinking.

3 **Can you think of another title for the poem?**
Answers will vary but should relate to Christmas Eve and/or the feeling of excitement.

4 **Did you like the text? Why? Why not?**
Answers will vary but encourage the children to explain their answers (e.g. *I liked it because it reminded me of Christmas*).

3 Explore

- Look at the poem's features together. Compare this poem with 'Eight Candles Burning'. Ask the children if they can remember the key features of a poem (e.g. line and verse). Discuss the rhyming words (there are more than in Unit 5). Draw the children's attention to any patterns. Encourage the children to identify the emotive language the poet has used and discuss it (e.g. 'terrible riot'; 'it keeps going round in my mind'; 'heavenly smell').
- Explore together the effect of the line 'But I've tried and I've tried and I've tried'. Ask the children why the poet uses this repetition. What effect does it have on the reader?

4 Skills focus

See pages 66 to 67

Use the information from the **Skills guide** and the relevant **Skills graphic** to introduce the skill of retrieval.

1 Model the skill using the **Unit 6 Modelling slides** and the **Modelling retrieval** guidance on page 66.

2 The children can then attempt the **Retrieval** questions on page 70.

3 Finally, the **Mix it up!** questions on page 71 offer practice in a range of comprehension skills.

Answers and marking guidance for all questions are included on pages 66 to 67.

5 Where next?

- Speaking and listening task: Using the linked text, 'Eight Candles Burning' (Unit 5), verbally compare and contrast the festival of Hanukkah with the festival of Christmas. Encourage the children to discuss the main similarities and differences. You could extend the discussion to include other winter festivals, especially if the children in your class celebrate other festivals at this time of year.
- Writing task: The children could write a diary entry imagining that something very exciting is happening the next day. They should use lots of emotive language, like that found in both 'Christmas Eve' and 'Eight Candles Burning'.

Reading list

Fiction

- *The Christmas Eve Tree* by Delia Huddy
- *The Night Before the Night Before Christmas* by Kes Gray
- *Refuge* by Anne Booth

Class reads

- *How Winston Delivered Christmas* by Alex T. Smith

Non-fiction

- *Walk this World at Christmas Time* by Debbie Powell

Poetry

- 'Eight Candles Burning' by Celia Warren (Linked text: Unit 5)
- ''Twas the Night Before Christmas' by Clement Clarke Moore

Films

- *Ten European Christmas Traditions* (CBBC *Newsround*, 2017)

Modelling retrieval

See Unit 6 Modelling slides

Use the **Skills guide** (see pages 16 to 17) and the downloadable **Skills graphic** to support your modelling.

1 **What is the poet trying to do?**

sleep

Read the question together and model identifying the key word 'trying' and scanning for it in the text. This looks like an easy question; however, the children may miss the key information by trying to comprehend the whole text. Once the children have found 'trying', continue by reading around the word to find the answer to the question.

2 **What is the poet thinking about? Give <u>two</u> things.**

The poet is thinking about Christmas the next day and all the presents he might be getting.

Read the question together and model identifying the key word 'thinking' and scanning for it in the text. Think aloud: *How many pieces of information do we need to find?* Continue by reading around the word 'thinking'. Some children may try to guess the answer to this question; if so, ensure all children use 'Fastest finger first' (see page 17) to prove that their answer is correct and taken from the text.

3 **Look at the fourth verse. What is keeping the poet awake here? Tick <u>one</u>.**

seeing presents ☐

hearing his parents ☐

smelling food ☑

the TV ☐

Read the question together and model using the locator to find the verse. Think aloud: *Does the poet say what is keeping him awake here?* The children may use ideas from other parts of the text to answer (e.g. hearing his parents in the second verse). If this happens, remind the children to use the locator as the question tells them exactly where to look.

4 **Why is the poet trying so hard to get to sleep?**

He thinks Father Christmas won't visit if he's awake.

Read the question together. This question requires an understanding of the whole text. If the children find this tricky, provide them with a locator for the penultimate verse. Think aloud: *What will happen if the poet doesn't go to sleep?* Once again, ensure that the children do not use their own knowledge to answer by asking them to point to the information in the text.

Retrieval questions mark scheme

See page 70

Answer	Guidance
1 trying to keep/be quiet	Some children may use ideas from later in the text (e.g. baking, or their own extrinsic knowledge such as watching TV). If so, model using the locator to support them to find the correct information. **Award 1 mark for any reference to trying to keep quiet.**
2 mince pies ☑ cake ☑	Some children may benefit from an additional locator to support their comprehension. Support the children to scan the text for the word 'baked' and any words from the same family ('bake', 'baking'). **Award 1 mark for the correct answers ticked.**

Answer		Guidance
3	Dad/Daddy/Father	If the children find this challenging, you may wish to provide a locator (e.g. verse 5). **Award 1 mark for any reference to Dad. Do not accept 'parents'.**
4	rolling around. ☑	The children may need support to use the locator. **Award 1 mark for the correct answer ticked.**
5	sheep	Some children may answer 'reindeer'. Support them to correct this by reminding them that the question says 'first' and encouraging them to reread the final verse. **Award 1 mark for the correct answer.**

Mix it up! questions mark scheme

See page 71

Answer		Guidance
1	can't stop thinking	Some children may respond vaguely (e.g. 'can't sleep'). Encourage the children to reread the text to find a more specific answer. **Award 1 mark for any reference to not being able to stop thinking.** Skill: Word meaning.
2	He's missed something off his list.	Some children's answers may refer to the whole poem (e.g. 'he's worried about getting to sleep'). If so, encourage them to use the locator to find the relevant part of the poem. **Award 1 mark for any reference to having missed something off his list.** Skill: Retrieval.
3	worried ☑	Encourage the children to verbally explain their answer, referring to the text. Some children may respond with 'angry', referring to the poet's frustration at not being able to sleep. If the children are able to explain this in relation to the text, then accept the answer. **Award 1 mark for the correct answer ticked.** Skill: Inference.
4	count reindeer	Some children may answer 'count sheep'. Reread the text together and point children to the last line to support them. **Award 1 mark for any reference to counting reindeer.** Skill: Sequencing.
5	Yes – counting reindeer will help him go to sleep. *OR* No – he is too excited to sleep.	Ideally, the children should link their answers to the ideas in the poem; however, references to extrinsic knowledge are acceptable (e.g. 'he will get too tired to stay awake'). **Award 1 mark for a plausible prediction.** Skill: Prediction.

Christmas Eve, by Brian Moses

This is a poem about the excitement children feel on Christmas Eve.

I'm trying to sleep on Christmas Eve
but I really can't settle down,
and I don't want to lie
with wide open eyes
till the morning comes around.

I hear Mum and Dad downstairs,
doing their best to keep quiet,
and although I'm in bed
with my favourite ted,
in my head there's a terrible riot.

I'm thinking of Christmas morning
and all the presents I'll find,
but what if I've missed
something good off my list,
it keeps going round in my mind.

Mum has been baking all day
making rolls, mince pies and cake,
and I know quite well
it's this heavenly smell
that's keeping me wide awake.

Now Dad says Father Christmas
won't leave any presents for me.
"Make no mistake,
if you're still awake,
he'll pass you by, you'll see!"

But I've tried and I've tried and I've tried
and I keep rolling round in my bed,
I still can't sleep,
and I'm fed up with sheep
so I'm counting reindeer instead!

Retrieval

Name: ______________________

1 Look at the second verse. What are Mum and Dad doing?

______________________ 1 mark

2 What things had Mum baked? Tick **two**.

buns ☐

loaves of bread ☐

mince pies ☐

cake ☐

1 mark

3 Who tells the poet that Father Christmas won't visit if he is awake?

______________________ 1 mark

4 Look at the last verse. What is the poet doing? Tick **one**.

The poet is ...

running up and down. ☐

going downstairs. ☐

rolling around. ☐

going to sleep. ☐

1 mark

5 Look at the last verse. What does the poet try counting first?

______________________ 1 mark

Mix it up!

Name: ____________________

1 Look at the third verse. What does *keeps going round in my mind* mean?

____________________ 1 mark

2 Look at the third verse. What is the poet worried about here?

____________________ 1 mark

3 Look at the fifth verse. How do you think the poet feels when his dad warns him about Father Christmas not visiting? Tick **one**.

sleepy ☐

sad ☐

angry ☐

worried ☐

1 mark

4 What does the poet do last to try to get to sleep?

____________________ 1 mark

5 Do you think the poet will be able to get to sleep? Tick **one**.

Yes ☐ No ☐

Why?

____

____

____________________ 1 mark

Ruby's Worry

by Tom Percival

Printable text Photocopiable text and questions • pages 73 to 75

Ruby's Worry is the story of a young girl, Ruby, who begins to worry. She is accompanied everywhere by her Worry, which becomes bigger as Ruby bottles up her feelings. However, she soon realises that everyone has Worries, and the more you talk about them, the smaller they become. This text is written by Tom Percival, the author of *Perfectly Norman*, the Unit 7 text. After both texts have been read, you may wish to discuss the links between them, exploring their similarities and differences with the children. **For guidance on running this task, see page 11.**

Progress check questions mark scheme

Answer	Guidance
1 kitchen/school bus/cinema	Some children may use other parts of the text to answer this question (e.g. 'breakfast'). If necessary, draw their attention to the locator and model using it to find the relevant paragraph. **Award 1 mark for 1 or more correct answers. Also accept references to the Worry going everywhere with Ruby.** Skill: Retrieval.
2 Ruby was perfectly happy. ✓	If necessary, emphasise that this question is looking for the event that happened *first*. Encourage the children to reread the text, scanning for key words such as 'perfectly happy' and 'discovered' – which comes first? **Award 1 mark for the correct answer ticked.** Skill: Sequencing.
3 (surprised)	If necessary, model reading around the meeting with the boy and using context clues, such as the fact that Ruby realises she is not the only person with a Worry. If the children respond with an incorrect option, encourage them to explain their thinking. **Award 1 mark for the correct answer circled. Accept other ways of showing the correct answer (e.g. ticked).** Skill: Inference.
4 strangest *OR* the strangest thing *OR* strangest thing *OR* strangest thing happened	If the children include additional words in their answer, read this question again as a group. Think aloud: *What is it asking for?* Emphasise that we only need **one** word and that word means something similar to 'unusual'. Which single word is it? **Award 1 mark for the correct answer. Accept any of the answers opposite as the children may not yet be confident with the expectations of 'find and copy' questions.** Skill: Word meaning.
5 Ruby tells the boy about her Worry. ✓	Whether their response is correct or not, encourage the children to verbally explain their answers to you. If their response is correct, this will give you valuable information about their understanding of prediction. If their response is incorrect, they may still be able to give a plausible explanation which shows understanding. In this case, refocus them on the question and emphasise 'most likely'. Think aloud: *Which option is more likely than the others?* **Award 1 mark for the correct answer ticked.** Skill: Prediction.

Progress check 1

Name: ______________________________

1 Look at the second paragraph. Where did the Worry go with Ruby?

______________________________ 1 mark

2 Which of these events happened first? Tick **one**.

Ruby saw a boy at the park. ☐

Ruby discovered her Worry. ☐

Ruby's Worry grew. ☐

Ruby was perfectly happy. ☐

1 mark

3 Ruby met a boy who also had a Worry. How do you think she felt when she met him? Circle **one**.

angry	surprised	upset	silly

1 mark

4 *She asked the boy what was on his mind and, as he told her, the strangest thing happened ... his Worry began to shrink!*
Find and copy **one** word that tells us that something unusual was happening.

______________________________ 1 mark

5 What do you think is most likely to happen next in the story? Tick **one**.

Ruby runs away from the boy. ☐

Ruby tells the boy about her Worry. ☐

The boy shouts at Ruby. ☐

Ruby's Worry gets even bigger. ☐

1 mark

Ruby's Worry, by Tom Percival

Have you ever been worried about something? Ruby has. This text is from *Ruby's Worry*, a story of how a girl called Ruby found out that everyone has worries, but if you talk about them, they begin to shrink!

Ruby was perfectly happy. Until one day ... she discovered a Worry. It wasn't a very *big* Worry ... In fact, it was so small that, at first, Ruby hardly noticed it. But then the Worry started to grow. Each day it got a little bit bigger ... It just wouldn't leave her alone. It was there at breakfast, staring at her over the cereal box. And it was STILL there at night, when she cleaned her teeth. The funny thing was that no one else could see Ruby's Worry – not even her teacher. So Ruby pretended that *she* couldn't see it either. She tried to carry on as if everything was normal – but it just wasn't! The Worry was *always* there – stopping her from doing the things that she loved.

Ruby wondered if the Worry would ever go away. What if it didn't? What if it stayed with her *forever*? Ruby didn't realise, but she was doing the worst thing you can ever do with a Worry ... she was worrying about it! Now the Worry was ENORMOUS! It could barely fit in the kitchen at teatime. It filled up half of the school bus ... and it took up whole rows at the cinema. The Worry became the only thing that Ruby could think about, and it seemed like she would never feel happy again.

Then, one day, something unexpected happened ... Ruby noticed a boy sitting alone at the park. He looked how she felt – sad. And then she noticed something else, something hovering next to him. Could it be ... a Worry? It was! Ruby realised that she wasn't the *only* person with a Worry after all. Other people had them too! She asked the boy what was on his mind and, as he told her, the strangest thing happened ... his Worry began to shrink!

Perfectly Norman

by Tom Percival

Printable text • Modelling slides Photocopiable text and questions • pages 80 to 83

Celebrating diversity and difference is such an important facet of education. This text emphasises that it's good to be different. It is a great way of encouraging children to see difference as a positive thing. Another text by the author Tom Percival, *Ruby's Worry*, appears in Progress check 1. You may wish to discuss the similarities and differences between the two texts once this unit has been completed.

1 Get ready

Discuss the **Key vocabulary** identified in the **Language toolkit** and then complete the vocabulary and phonics activities as desired. Please note that the selected vocabulary is a guide. Depending on the needs of your cohort, additional vocabulary discussion may be beneficial before, during and after reading. Next, display the text (pages 80 to 81) so the children can see the title and any illustrations, and encourage the children to discuss the following questions before reading.

1 What type of text is this? How do you know?
The children should be able to recognise this as a fiction text and explain its features (e.g. *there is an illustration*; *real people do not have wings*).

2 What does it mean to be 'normal'?
Answers will vary but many children should be able to give an opinion. Explain that there is no such thing as a 'normal' person by pointing out that we are all different and that this is a good thing because it makes life more interesting.

3 What's different about you?
Answers will vary depending on what the children see as different. You may wish to start off with neutral differences in appearance (e.g. eye colour or being right-/left-handed) and then move on to likes and dislikes. Emphasis needs to be placed on these differences being positive and how they make you 'you'.

4 Have you ever tried to hide something about yourself?
Answers will vary. Hopefully none of the children have ever felt they needed to hide something but this is a good introduction to the concept of the story to come.

Language toolkit

Key vocabulary

extraordinary	hesitantly	imagined
normal	notice	perfectly
problematic	tatty	unbearable

Vocabulary discussion questions

- If something is **perfectly normal**, what does that mean? Is a yellow elephant ordinary or **extraordinary**?
- Have you ever used something so much it became **tatty**? What was it?
- Have you ever done something **hesitantly**?

Vocabulary activities

1 The word 'bearable' is turned into **unbearable** by adding the prefix 'un–' which means 'not'. Can the children think of any other words that start in the same way (e.g. 'uncomfortable')?

2 Use one of the vocabulary activities on page 15 to investigate some of the key words above.

Phonics

–ly suffix	**finally, hesitantly, nervously, perfectly**
Longer words	**extraordinary, miserable, problematic, uncomfortable**
Common exception words	**any, bath, children, could, great, most, old, only, parents, people, should, would**

Phonics activity

How many past tense verbs can the children spot? You may wish to remind the children that most past tense verbs end with the suffix '–ed' (e.g. **compared**).

2 First steps

Read the text together and then encourage the children to discuss the following questions.

1 **What is the main character called? Which other characters appear in the story?**
Norman. Norman's mum and dad; the boy that tried to take Norman's coat off; other children wearing coats/ with wings. Some children may answer 'Perfectly Norman' – if so, discuss whether that is his actual name and ask the children whether there is a clue in the story that tells us that it's not.

2 **What happens to Norman at the beginning of the story?**
He grows a pair of wings, flies in the air and feels extraordinary. Some children may try to tell you what happens next but focus them on the word 'beginning'.

3 **What happens at the very end of the story?**
Norman loves his wings and encourages other children to take off their coats and show their wings too.

4 **Did you like the text? Why? Why not?**
Answers will vary but encourage the children to explain their answers (e.g. *I liked it because Norman was happy and loved his wings in the end*).

3 Explore

- Discuss what it would be like to suddenly grow a pair of wings. Would the children feel the same as Norman? What would they do? What would be good about having a pair of wings? Would there be anything problematic about it?
- The author makes Norman seem a little bit like a superhero – his ability to fly is his superpower. Say to the children: *Let's imagine that everyone here is a superhero. What would your superpower be?* Discuss the answers the children come up with.
- The author repeatedly uses the word 'perfectly' in the text. Ask the children why they think the author talked about Norman being 'perfectly normal' at the beginning of the story and 'perfectly Norman' at the end of the story.

4 Skills focus

See pages 78 to 79

Use the information from the **Skills guide** and the relevant **Skills graphic** to introduce the skill of inference.

1 Model the skill using the **Unit 7 Modelling slides** and the **Modelling inference** guidance on page 78.

2 The children can then attempt the **Inference** questions on page 82.

3 Finally, the **Mix it up!** questions on page 83 offer practice in a range of comprehension skills.

Answers and marking guidance for all questions are included on pages 78 to 79.

5 Where next?

- Speaking and listening task: Work with the children to design and create a worry monster for the classroom. Encourage them to talk about their worries, write or draw them, and finally 'feed' them to the monster to make them shrink and disappear.
- Writing task: The children could write a postcard to someone else, offering to listen to their worries. This could be completed as a class, where every child is paired up carefully with another child, or more widely, involving relatives and siblings.

Reading list

Fiction

- *The Koala Who Could* by Rachel Bright
- *Ruby's Worry* by Tom Percival
(Linked text: Progress check 1)
- *Silly Billy* by Anthony Browne

Class reads

- *Worries Go Away!* By Kes Gray

Non-fiction

- *In My Heart: A Book of Feelings* by Jo Witek
- *No Worries* by Katie Abey

Poetry

- *A is Amazing* by Wendy Cooling
- *I'm Not Afraid of Spiders: Poems About Feelings* by Jane Rogers

Films

- *Inside Out* (Walt Disney Pictures, 2015)

Modelling inference

See Unit 7 Modelling slides

Use the **Skills guide** (see pages 20 to 21) and the downloadable **Skills graphic** to support your modelling.

1 ***Soon Norman was swooping around and generally having the MOST. FUN. EVER!*** **How do you think Norman felt when he first grew his wings? Tick one.**

worried ☐

excited ☑

sad ☐

angry ☐

Read the question together and model using the locator and key words to support finding the clues needed to make an inference. Explore the possible answers together and point out that they are all feelings. Ask the children how they would feel if they were having 'the most fun ever'. Some children may use their knowledge of the latter part of the text and answer 'worried' or 'sad'. If so, remind them that a key word in the question is 'first' and that they should use the locator to help them find the answer.

2 **Why do you think Norman did not show his wings to his parents?**

Norman didn't show his wings because he was embarrassed/worried.

Read the question together. As this question does not have a locator, model identifying the key word 'parents' and scanning the text to find the appropriate section. Focus the discussion on how Norman is feeling at this point in the story. Think aloud: *If you were Norman, would you want to show your parents? Why? Why not?* Discuss the possible reasons Norman might not show his wings to his parents (e.g. because his wings made him different; he thought his parents might not like them).

3 ***The only time that Norman could feel normal now was when it rained.*** **Why do you think Norman felt better when it rained?**

Everyone wore their coats, so it did not look strange for Norman to be wearing his coat too.

Read the question together and model using the locator to find the relevant section. Read the sentences preceding the locator, which tell us when Norman finds it difficult to wear a coat. Discuss what might be different when it rains. Think aloud: *What do people usually wear when it rains? Why might that make Norman feel better?* If the children try to use their extrinsic knowledge, remind them to link their answer to the text.

4 **How do you think Norman felt when he saw the other children wearing their coats? Why?**

He felt upset and wanted to help them because those children were hiding their wings and did not feel able to fly in the air like him.

Read the question together and point out that it has two parts. The children are likely to be able to decide upon a feeling relatively easily but may need support to formulate a reason why. If the children think that he is happy, refocus the discussion by thinking aloud: *How did Norman feel when he was wearing his coat?* Encourage them to consider how the other children wearing coats might feel.

Inference questions mark scheme

See page 82

Answer	Guidance
1 He was hiding his wings. ☑	Some children may use their extrinsic knowledge and choose another option here. In this case, remind them that this is an inference question so we need to find the clues in the text. **Award 1 mark for the correct answer ticked.**
2 sad/embarrassed/ashamed	Some children may concentrate on Norman's comfort rather than his emotions. If so, refocus them on to his feelings. **Award 1 mark for any reference to a plausible emotion. Also accept references to being uncomfortable.**

Answer		Guidance
3	excited/happy/free	Again, some children may concentrate on Norman's comfort rather than his emotions. If so, refocus them on to his feelings. **Award 1 mark for any reference to a plausible emotion. Also accept references to him feeling like himself.**
4	Norman was brave./They wanted to fly too.	If the children need additional support for this question, scaffold them by asking what the other children might be thinking about Norman or how the other children might be feeling. **Award 1 mark for any reference that shows understanding of the text, either about Norman or about how the other children were feeling.**
5	Because he was being himself/free/didn't need to hide any more/liked his wings.	Some children may respond by saying that Norman is able to fly, but he can do that throughout the story. In this case, refocus the children by asking what has changed by the end of the story. **Award 1 mark for any reference to Norman being himself or not needing/wanting to hide any more.**

Mix it up! questions mark scheme

See page 83

Answer		Guidance
1	test *OR* to test them out *OR* test them out *OR* test them	If the children give more than one word as the answer, refocus them on the word 'one'. Discuss which word means 'tried' or 'tried out'. Some children may answer 'flew' from elsewhere in the text. This should not be accepted, but refocus the children on the locator in the question to support them. **Award 1 mark for the correct answer.** Skill: Word meaning.
2	scared/worried/embarrassed	Some children may think that he is still excited by his wings. In this case, refocus them on the sentence beginning 'As he went in …'. Think aloud: *The text tells us he covered himself up so his parents didn't notice. What inference can we make from this?* Encourage the children to discuss why Norman might cover his wings. **Award 1 mark for any reference to a plausible emotion. Do not accept simple references to sadness.** Skill: Inference.
3	swimming pool ✓ park ✓	Some children may attempt to use inference and assume that Norman is at school when he sees other children or when the boy tries to pull off his coat. In this case, remind them that this is a retrieval question and prompt them to scan the text for the answer options given in the question. **Award 1 mark for the correct answers ticked.** Skill: Retrieval.
4	He flew.	Some children may say that Norman smiled, which is from just before he removes his coat. If so, encourage them to find where Norman takes off his coat and read the immediate sentences after this to find what he does first. **Award 1 mark for any reference to flying. Also accept a direct quote from the text (e.g. 'he leapt into the air'; 'he let his … wings fan out').** Skill: Sequencing.
5	No – because he is not worried about them any more. *OR* Yes – if someone is mean to him about them.	If the children need additional support, encourage them to put themselves in Norman's shoes. **Award 1 mark for a plausible prediction.** Skill: Prediction.

Perfectly Norman, by Tom Percival

This is an extract from a story about a boy called Norman who grows a pair of wings. At first, he is worried because his wings make him different from everyone else.

Norman had always been normal – *perfectly* normal. Until one day ... he grew a pair of wings! Norman had imagined growing taller ... or growing a beard like his dad ... but he *never* imagined growing a pair of wings! Still, they were here now, so he decided to test them out right away. Soon Norman was swooping around and generally having the MOST. FUN. EVER! But then ... he had to go in for dinner.

You see, Norman had always been SO normal he didn't know how his parents would feel about his *extraordinary* wings. As he went in, Norman covered himself up in a great big coat. His parents didn't notice the wings ... But they *did* think it was odd to be wearing a coat indoors!

Bath time was problematic. So was bedtime. The coat was hot and uncomfortable, but Norman had decided that no one should see his wings – ever. The next day Norman went to the park, but he was far too hot to play any of his favourite games. And so it went on ... Long car journeys were unbearable, the swimming pool was dreadful, and that was *nothing* compared to his friend's birthday party. The only time that Norman could feel normal now was when it rained.

One day a boy tried to pull his coat off, and Norman had to run away – hot-faced, angry and sad. He wished he'd *never* grown those stupid wings. Then he saw some birds, high up in the sky, and remembered the joy of his first flight. It occurred to Norman that it was the *coat* that was making him miserable, *not* the *wings*. "Why don't you take that tatty old thing off?" suggested his mum and dad. Norman looked up at them hesitantly. His parents smiled and nodded. Norman smiled back. Then he threw off the coat ... and let his wonderful wings fan out. Norman leapt into the air ...

Finally he was free of that coat! He noticed a few other children wearing thick, heavy coats of their own. They looked up at Norman and round at each other nervously. There was a moment's pause and then ... WHOOSH! The sky was filled with flying people! Norman had never felt SO happy. He realised that there was no such thing as *perfectly normal* ... But he was *perfectly Norman*. Which was just as it should be.

Inference

Name: ____________________

1 Why did Norman wear a coat everywhere? Tick **one**.

He was cold. ☐

He liked his coat. ☐

He was hiding his wings. ☐

It was raining. ☐

1 mark

2 How do you think Norman felt while he was hiding his wings?

____

1 mark

3 Look at the fourth paragraph. How do you think Norman felt when he took off his coat?

____

1 mark

4 Look at the last paragraph. What do you think the children thought when they saw Norman flying without his coat?

____

1 mark

5 *Norman had never felt SO happy.*
Why do you think he felt so happy at the end of the story?

____

____

1 mark

Mix it up!

Name: ______________________________

1 *Still, they were here now, so he decided to test them out right away.*
Find and copy **one** word that tells you Norman tried his wings out.

____

1 mark

2 Look at the first paragraph. How do you think Norman felt when he had to go in for dinner?

____

1 mark

3 Look at the third paragraph. Where did Norman wear his coat? Tick **two**.

swimming pool ☐

school ☐

park ☐

shop ☐

1 mark

4 Look at the fourth paragraph. After he took off his coat, what did Norman do first?

____

1 mark

5 Do you think Norman will ever hide his wings again? Tick **one**.

Yes ☐ No ☐

Why?

____

____

____

1 mark

Sir Charlie Stinky Socks: The Really Big Adventure by Kristina Stephenson

Printable text • Modelling slides   Photocopiable text and questions • pages 88 to 91

Knights, castles and magical settings have long fascinated children. This text is an extract from a longer story about the adventures of the brave knight, Sir Charlie Stinky Socks. The author has written a number of books featuring Sir Charlie and you may wish to encourage children to read his further adventures. This text is the first of two that feature dragons (see also *The Night Dragon* in Unit 9). You may wish to make links between the texts once both units have been completed.

1 Get ready

Discuss the **Key vocabulary** identified in the **Language toolkit** and then complete the vocabulary and phonics activities as desired. Please note that the selected vocabulary is a guide. Depending on the needs of your cohort, additional vocabulary discussion may be beneficial before, during and after reading. Next, display the text (pages 88 to 89) so the children can see the title and any illustrations, and encourage the children to discuss the following questions before reading.

1. What type of text is this? How do you know?
   The children should be able to recognise this as a fiction text and explain its features.
2. This story is an adventure story. Who has been on an adventure? What happened?
   Answers will vary but almost all the children should be able to relate to the idea of going on an adventure.
3. What kinds of characters do we usually find in fairy tales?
   Answers will vary but all the children should be able to contribute. Some may name specific characters (e.g. Cinderella) but try to group them together into categories (e.g. heroes, villains, royalty).
4. Have you ever read stories that have knights and castles in them?
   Answers will vary depending on the children's exposure to texts but many should be able to name at least one traditional tale (e.g. 'Sleeping Beauty', 'Rapunzel').

Language toolkit

Key vocabulary

fearless	fearsome	hideous
monstrous	mounted	quivered
rallied	scarpered	shivered
soothe	trusty	whispered

Vocabulary discussion questions

- Are all monsters **monstrous**?
- When have you been **fearless**?
- Do you only **shiver** when you're cold?

Vocabulary activities

1. Can the children explain the difference between being **fearless** and **fearsome**? Explore the root word 'fear' and the suffixes '–less' and '–some'.
2. Use drama to explore verbs such as **shivered**, **quivered**, **whispered**, **soothe**, **scarpered** and **rallied**.

Phonics

–ed suffix	covered, followed, groaned, moaned, mounted, packed, picked, quivered, rallied, rescued, scared, scarpered, shivered, smiled, stared, trembled, whispered
Longer words	adventure, envelope, sandwiches
Common exception words	again, last

Phonics activity

How many rhyming words can the children find?

2 First steps

Read the text together and then encourage the children to discuss the following questions.

1 **Where is the story set?**
The story is mainly set in the deep, dark forest; however, at the end of the text Sir Charlie finds a tall tower in a clearing.

2 **Sir Charlie Stinky Socks is the main character in the story, but which other characters also appear?**
Envelope the cat; the good grey mare; the witch; the terrible beasties, the wiggly woos and the dragon.

3 **What did Sir Charlie have to escape from in the deep, dark forest?**
The terrible beasties.

4 **Did you like the text? Why? Why not?**
Answers will vary but encourage the children to explain their answers (e.g. *I liked it because Sir Charlie went on lots of adventures and I'd like to know where he goes next*).

3 Explore

- Discuss the other texts that the children have read that include knights (see the **Reading list** for some examples). What are knights famous for? What do they usually do in stories? Are they always male? From this, discuss what other adventures Sir Charlie Stinky Socks might go on.
- The author uses a wide range of language features in the story. Explore these features with the children and encourage them to find examples from the text: rhyming pairs (e.g. 'shivered and quivered'); alliteration (e.g. 'the witch with the watch'; 'frightful and fearsome'; 'hairy, hideous creatures'); and personification (e.g. 'trees moaning'; 'the sun threw down its light').

4 Skills focus

See pages 86 to 87

Use the information from the **Skills guide** and the relevant **Skills graphic** to introduce the skill of sequencing.

1 Model the skill using the **Unit 8 Modelling slides** and the **Modelling sequencing** guidance on page 86.

2 The children can then attempt the **Sequencing** questions on page 90.

3 Finally, the **Mix it up!** questions on page 91 offer practice in a range of comprehension skills.

Answers and marking guidance for all questions are included on pages 86 to 87.

5 Where next?

- Speaking and listening task: Discuss the characters with the children. Sir Charlie is very brave and courageous but some of the other characters (Envelope, the good grey mare and the witch) are very scared of the dark forest, the terrible beasties and the wiggly woos. Pretend to be one of the scared characters: can the children give you some words of encouragement? The children may also remember the text from Progress check 1, *Ruby's Worry*, which may give them some ideas about how to cope when they're scared or worried.
- Writing task: The children could write their own ending to the story. What happens between Sir Charlie and the fearsome dragon? Does Sir Charlie go on another really big adventure? The children could then compare it with the real ending of the book.

Reading list

Fiction

- *The Dragon and the Nibblesome Knight* by Elli Woollard
- *The Knight Who Said "No!"* by Lucy Rowland
- *The Knight Who Wouldn't Fight* by Helen Docherty
- *The Night Dragon* by Naomi Howarth (Linked text: Unit 9)

Class reads

- *Sir Charlie Stinky Socks* series by Kristina Stephenson

Non-fiction

- *See Inside Castles* by Katie Daynes

Poetry

- *Dragon Poems* by John Foster

Films

- *George and the Dragon* (British Council, 2014)

TV series

- *'The Snow Dragon', Jackanory Junior* (CBeebies, 2012)

Modelling sequencing

See Unit 8 Modelling slides

Use the **Skills guide** (see pages 18 to 19) and the downloadable **Skills graphic** to support your modelling.

1 Look at the second paragraph. What did Envelope do first after they got to the forest? Circle one.

(shivered) | hid | jumped | scarpered

Read the question together and model using the locator to find the relevant paragraph. Then model scanning the paragraph for the key word 'Envelope'. Encourage the children to read this sentence and the one before to check what Envelope does first after they reach the forest. Model finding the word 'shivered' in the answer options and circling it.

2 What did Sir Charlie do first to the terrible beasties?

He sang them a lullaby.

Read the question together. This question does not have a locator so be sure to model finding the key words 'terrible beasties' and scanning the text to find the appropriate section. Once you have found it, remind the children that the question asks us what Sir Charlie does 'first' to the terrible beasties and model reading on to find the answer.

3 Look at the last paragraph. Where was Sir Charlie standing at the end of the text?

a clearing

Read the question together and model using the locator to find the relevant paragraph. The children may initially answer 'the tower'. If so, reread the paragraph together. Think aloud: *Does the text say Sir Charlie went to the tower or that he saw the tower from the clearing?* If necessary, demonstrate this with a quick sketch.

4 Number the events to show the order in which they happened in the story. One has been done for you.

Sir Charlie saw the dragon.	5
Sir Charlie cut up his sandwiches.	3
Sir Charlie sang his lullaby.	2
Sir Charlie packed for his trip.	1
Sir Charlie found a tall tower.	4

Read the question together. The children need to understand the text as a whole in order to respond correctly. If they are struggling, provide cut-up sections of the story and help them to physically order the sections first. Then model numbering the statements in the question and checking the order is correct by using the text.

Sequencing questions mark scheme

See page 90

Answer	Guidance
1 water 3 sandwiches 2 sword 1 favourite little something 4	Remind the children to use the locator to find the relevant information. Some children may find 'sword' challenging to order as the text says he picked the sword rather than packed it. **Award 1 mark for the correct numbers in all boxes.**
2 (trembled)	If the children need additional support to answer this question, remind them to scan the text for references to the witch. They could then highlight these references to support them to answer correctly. **Award 1 mark for the correct answer circled.**
3 The trees stopped groaning. ✓	There are only two options here as the language is very similar and the children will need to read the text closely to answer the question. **Award 1 mark for the correct answer ticked.**

Answer		Guidance
4	he drew his sword/smiled/cut up his sandwiches for the beasties/did not turn/did not run	If the children need additional support for this question, provide them with a paragraph locator or, if needed, a sentence locator (e.g. *Look at the sentence that begins 'Instead…'*). You may need to discuss the meaning of the phrase 'as soon as'. **Award 1 mark for a reference to something Sir Charlie did. Also accept answers referring to him *not* turning and *not* running.**
5	the clearing [3] the deep, dark forest [2] the hills [1] the tower [4]	The children may miss the reference in the first paragraph to 'Over the hills'. In this case, remind them to scan the text for the key words in the question. **Award 1 mark for the correct numbers in all boxes.**

Mix it up! questions mark scheme

See page 91

Answer		Guidance
1	Sssshhhhhh!	If the children respond with another thing Sir Charlie says, refocus them on the word 'first'. Think aloud: *Can we find the first thing he says?* **Award 1 mark for the correct answer. Accept any spelling.** **Skill: Sequencing.**
2	6/six	If the children find this tricky, remind them that this is a retrieval question which means the answer is right there in the text. Explain that 'how many' gives us a clue that we are looking for a number. Support them to scan the text to find the relevant information. **Award 1 mark for a correct answer.** **Skill: Retrieval.**
3	scarpered *OR* fled	By this point, the children should understand how to approach 'find and copy' questions. If the children give more than one word as the answer, refocus them on the word 'one'. Discuss which words mean 'ran away'. **Award 1 mark for a correct answer.** **Skill: Word meaning.**
4	proud	Some children may answer with a vague emotion (e.g. 'happy'). Although this is technically correct, encourage them to explain their answer to prove their understanding (e.g. *Happy because he's managed to save himself and his animals from the monsters*). **Award 1 mark for any reference to a plausible emotion.** **Skill: Inference.**
5	Sir Charlie fights the dragon. [✓]	If the children give another response, encourage them to justify their prediction using the text to check their understanding. Focus the children on the clues the text gives us to predict (e.g. Think aloud: *It's unlikely that Envelope will scare the dragon because the cat has been scared throughout the text and you would need to be brave to scare the fearsome dragon*). **Award 1 mark for the correct answer ticked.** **Skill: Prediction.**

Sir Charlie Stinky Socks: The Really Big Adventure, by Kristina Stephenson

This is an extract from *Sir Charlie Stinky Socks: The Really Big Adventure*, a story of a brave knight who goes on an epic adventure through the deep, dark forest. What dangers await Sir Charlie and his faithful pet cat, Envelope?

Sir Charlie picked his best sword, packed some sandwiches, a big bottle of water and a favourite little something for the journey (just in case). And with a song in his heart he mounted his good grey mare. Over the hills and far away rode Sir Charlie and his cat. (Oh, and a wily witch with a watch followed behind on a broom.)

At last they came to a deep, dark forest, where monstrous trees groaned and terrible beasties moaned. Envelope shivered. The good grey mare quivered. (While the witch with the watch covered her eyes.) But brave Sir Charlie stood steady in his boots. "Sssshhhhhh!" he whispered into the woods. "Tis I ... Sir Charlie Stinky Socks with a song to soothe you." And as Sir Charlie sang his lullaby the trees stopped groaning. But the terrible beasties went on moaning.

"Stop your moaning," cried the knight. "Come out and eat me if you dare!" Out of the darkness crept six slobbering beasties. That fearless cat, Envelope, scarpered! The good grey mare fled! (And even the wily witch with the watch trembled behind a tree.) But bold Sir Charlie did not turn. Brave Sir Charlie did not run. Instead he drew his trusty sword and did what any good knight would do ... he smiled and cut up his sandwiches!

The beasties stood and stared. They were hairy, hideous creatures indeed, but they were more scared of Sir Charlie Stinky Socks than he was of them! Charlie fed the beasties and the beasties stopped moaning. (And the wily witch with the watch looked on with a grin and checked the time.) But this was no way to end a really big adventure. So Sir Charlie Stinky Socks rescued his cat, rallied his good grey mare and set off once again, never minding the wiggly woos who waited in the grass or the six not so terrible beasties who followed him.

The forest grew thicker and the bushes became thorny. Lucky for Envelope and the good grey mare that Sir Charlie Stinky Socks led the way with his trusty sword. It was thirsty work for a bold, brave knight; how glad he was to have a big bottle of water by his side. And then, at last, they came to a clearing in the trees where the sun threw down its pale yellow light ... onto a tall tower with ... a pointy roof. But it also threw its light onto ... a long, green dragon! He was frightful and fearsome and coughing out fire while he stomped in a temper around the tower. *Ha ha!* thought Sir Charlie Stinky Socks. *Just the thing for a really big adventure!*

Sequencing

Name: ____________________

1 Look at the first sentence. Number the items to show the order in which Sir Charlie packed them. One has been done for you.

water	☐
sandwiches	2
sword	☐
favourite little something	☐

1 mark

2 What was the third thing the witch did in the story? Circle **one**.

followed Sir Charlie	checked the time	grinned	trembled

1 mark

3 Look at the sentence beginning *And as Sir Charlie sang ...* . Which of these events happened first? Tick **one**.

The trees stopped groaning.	☐
The beasties stopped moaning.	☐

1 mark

4 What did Sir Charlie do as soon as the six beasties crept out?

____

1 mark

5 Number the places to show the order in which they appear in the story. One has been done for you.

the clearing	☐
the deep, dark forest	☐
the hills	☐
the tower	4

1 mark

Mix it up!

Name: ____________________

1 Look at the second paragraph. What did Sir Charlie say first to the beasties?

____________________ 1 mark

2 Look at the third paragraph. How many slobbering beasties came out of the darkness?

____________________ 1 mark

3 Look at the third paragraph. Find and copy **one** word that means the same as 'ran away'.

____________________ 1 mark

4 How do you think Sir Charlie felt when the beasties stopped moaning?

____________________ 1 mark

5 What do you think is most likely to happen next? Tick **one**.

Sir Charlie runs away. ☐

Sir Charlie fights the dragon. ☐

Envelope scares the dragon away. ☐

The witch puts a spell on Sir Charlie. ☐

1 mark

The Night Dragon

by Naomi Howarth

Printable text • Modelling slides   Photocopiable text and questions • pages 96 to 99

With their links to myths and magic, dragons hold a fascination for many children. This text is an extract from a story about Maud, a 'night dragon' who needs a confidence boost. The text is the second of two stories that feature dragons, following on from the dragon we encountered at the end of *Sir Charlie Stinky Socks* in Unit 8. When making links between the two texts, you may wish to encourage the children to compare the two portrayals of dragons, as they are quite different.

1 Get ready

Discuss the **Key vocabulary** identified in the **Language toolkit** and then complete the vocabulary and phonics activities as desired. Please note that the selected vocabulary is a guide. Depending on the needs of your cohort, additional vocabulary discussion may be beneficial before, during and after reading. Next, display the text (pages 96 to 97) so the children can see the title and any illustrations, and encourage the children to discuss the following questions before reading.

1 **What type of text is this? How do you know?**
The children should be able to recognise this as a fiction text and explain its features.

2 **This story is about a night dragon. Which other books have you read that feature dragons?**
Answers will vary depending on the children's exposure to texts but all should be able to make a link to the dragon in *Sir Charlie Stinky Socks* if Unit 8 has been completed.

3 **In stories, are dragons usually heroes or villains? Why do you think this is?**
Answers will vary depending on the texts the children have encountered. However, it is likely that they will favour casting dragons as villains. Regardless of their answer, encourage discussion about a range of portrayals of dragons and make comparisons between them.

4 **How do you think the night dragon is going to be similar or different to other dragons you have seen?**
Answers will vary but may focus on the illustration or the use of 'night' in the title of the text.

Language toolkit

Key vocabulary

bother	brute	cackled
cast	covered	croaked
insisted	nightfall	snarled
soaring	unshakeable	weedy

Vocabulary discussion questions

- A witch can **cast** a spell. Can you **cast** anything else?
- If you are a **brute**, can you be **weedy**?
- Have you ever had an **unshakeable** feeling?

Vocabulary activities

1 Ask the children to talk in the same ways as the characters: **snarled**, **croaked**, **cackled** and **insisted**.

2 Complete a 'Shades of meaning' activity (see page 15) with the children using **weedy** at one end and **brute** at the other.

Phonics

–ed suffix	decided, invited, lived, shouted, squeaked, stepped, tried, whispered
Longer words	together, unshakeable
Common exception words	could, every, only, pretty, would

Phonics activity

Can the children find all the past tense verbs with the suffix '–ed'? Can they sort them into their different rules?

2 First steps

Read the text together and then encourage the children to discuss the following questions.

1. **Who is the main character in the story? What are they?**
   Maud. She's a dragon.

2. **Where do the dragons in this story live?**
   In a land far away on top of a very high mountain.

3. **What important job does a night dragon do? Why is it important?**
   They bring night-time to the sky every night. It is important so that we can rest/so that nocturnal animals know to get up.

4. **Did you like the text? Why? Why not?**
   Answers will vary but encourage the children to explain their answers (e.g. *I liked it because Maud managed to fly just like the other night dragons*).

3 Explore

- The night dragons are unkind to Maud because she is different to them. Explore the contrast between how Maud and Mouse behave and the behaviour of the other night dragons. For example, Mouse is reassuring to Maud; however, the other night dragons snarl and shout at her. As we saw with Unit 7 in *Perfectly Norman*, being different is a positive thing. Discuss what we should do to support a friend if someone else says mean things to them.

- The author uses lots of descriptive language in this text (e.g. 'swoop into the air, breathing huge flames of fire'). Discuss how phrases and sentences like this affect the reader.

4 Skills focus

See pages 94 to 95

Use the information from the **Skills guide** and the relevant **Skills graphic** to introduce the skill of inference.

1. Model the skill using the **Unit 9 Modelling slides** and the **Modelling inference** guidance on page 94.

2. The children can then attempt the **Inference** questions on page 98.

3. Finally, the **Mix it up!** questions on page 99 offer practice in a range of comprehension skills.

Answers and marking guidance for all questions are included on pages 94 to 95.

5 Where next?

- Speaking and listening task: Share an experience or time when you lacked confidence. Discuss whether the children have ever felt unconfident about something and still managed to succeed. How did they get over their fear? Who can help us to become more confident? Discuss what we feel less confident about now and how we can help each other. Decide upon a list of classroom confidence boosts that everyone can use to support each other (e.g. saying what a good job someone is doing; praising somebody for trying their best).

- Writing task: The children could write a congratulatory card to Maud, celebrating her success at flying. They could also add confidence-boosting messages to help her to become a true night dragon.

Reading list

Fiction

- *The Dragon Machine* by Helen Ward
- *The Egg* by M. P. Robertson
- *George and the Dragon* by Christopher Wormell
- *Sir Charlie Stinky Socks: The Really Big Adventure* by Kristina Stephenson (Linked text: Unit 8)

Class reads

- *Tell Me a Dragon* by Jackie Morris

Non-fiction

- *National Geographic Kids: Real Dragons* by Jennifer Szymanski

Poetry

- *Evidence of Dragons* by Pie Corbett

Films

- *Pete's Dragon* (Walt Disney Pictures, 2016)

Modelling inference

See Unit 9 Modelling slides

Use the **Skills guide** (see pages 20 to 21) and the downloadable **Skills graphic** to support your modelling.

1 Look at the second paragraph. How do you think Maud felt when the night dragons swooped into the air?

left out

Read the question together and model using the locator to find the relevant paragraph. Discuss what we know from the text (e.g. that all the other dragons were in the air breathing clouds of smoke to bring on night). Next, model making inferences from the text and using extrinsic knowledge to move the discussion on towards identifying Maud's feelings. Think aloud: *How would we feel if we were the only ones who couldn't do something?* Discuss how Maud is feeling (e.g. 'upset; left out because she's not a night dragon') and model writing an answer.

2 Why do you think Mouse told Maud she did not need to be big and scary?

to cheer her up

Read the question together. As this question does not have a locator, model identifying the key words 'Mouse', 'big' and 'scary', and scanning the text for them. Some children may find this question challenging, so it is important to model thinking between the lines of the text here. Think aloud: *How would you feel if your friend was saying nice things to you when you were feeling bad about yourself?*

3 How did Maud feel when she wasn't invited to the party? Tick one.

lonely ☑ angry ☐ happy ☐ surprised ☐

Read the question together. Like **question 2** above, this question does not have a locator so model identifying the key word 'invited' and scanning the text for it. Read the relevant sentence. Think aloud: *How would you feel if you were the only person not invited to a party?* Some children may argue that Maud would be angry. If so, refocus them on the clues in the text. Think aloud: *Are there any clues that show she is angry?* Finally, model ticking one answer only.

4 Do you think that Maud will be able to become a real night dragon? Explain your answer.

Yes – because she gets braver and learns to fly so in time she could learn to breathe smoke and make night come.

Read the question together. This is quite a complex inference to make so it is important to encourage the children to discuss what they know from the text before answering. You could go back to the beginning of the text and discuss the attributes of a night dragon (e.g. tough, flying, breathing fire, etc.) and whether Maud has any of these by the end of the text. Think aloud: *What does that tell us about Maud?* Encourage the children to use this information to help answer the question.

Inference questions mark scheme

See page 98

Answer	Guidance
1 because she is not like the other dragons/ because she cannot fly/because she cannot breathe fire	Some children may benefit from having a locator (e.g. 'I'll never be a night dragon!') to support them with this question. **Award 1 mark for any reference to her not being like the other dragons or any reference to the things she cannot do (e.g. fly, breathe fire).**
2 She was not a real night dragon. ☑	Some children may benefit from having a locator to support them with this question. Some may answer 'She was a special dragon' as that relates to your conversations around difference. In this case, refocus the children on to the conversation between Maud and the other dragons. Think aloud: *Were they all saying nice things to her?* **Award 1 mark for the correct answer ticked.**

Answer		Guidance
3	Night-time won't come.	If the children refer to the dragons being unable to breathe fire and make clouds, encourage them to expand their answer and think about the main function of a night dragon (to bring on night-time). **Award 1 mark for any reference to night-time not coming. Also accept any reference to the dragons being unable to use their other powers.**
4	terrified/scared/worried	If the children find this challenging, encourage them to put themselves in Maud's shoes and ask them how they would feel. **Award 1 mark for any reference to a plausible emotion. Also accept 'brave' if the answer includes an explanation of the reasoning (e.g. 'she's feeling brave because she knows she can do it').**
5	proud ✓	The children may answer 'scared' due to Maud's earlier tumble. In this case, refocus them on the key word 'flying' in the question. **Award 1 mark for the correct answer ticked.**

Mix it up! questions mark scheme

See page 99

Answer		Guidance
1	4/four	The children may answer '5' but this is incorrect. If so, refocus them on the phrase 'Maud was one of five dragons'. Think aloud: *That means there were five dragons in total, including Maud.* **Award 1 mark for a correct answer.** **Skill: Retrieval.**
2	annoyed/angry/protective	Some children may benefit from being given a locator to support them. If they answer 'upset' or 'sad', ask them to put themselves in Mouse's shoes. Think aloud: *If four people were saying mean things to your best friend, how would you feel? Would you just be upset, or something bigger?* **Award 1 mark for any reference to a plausible emotion.** **Skill: Inference.**
3	looked ✓	Support the children to use the locator if needed. Remind them of the strategies we use for definition (e.g. substitution). **Award 1 mark for the correct answer ticked.** **Skill: Word meaning.**
4	The other dragons called Maud names. 1 Maud flew in the air. 4 The other dragons had a party. 2 Maud stepped off the mountain. 3	The children need to understand the whole story to respond correctly. If they find this question challenging, remind them to scan the text for key words from each statement and highlight them. This will support them to work out the order. **Award 1 mark for the correct numbers in all boxes.** **Skill: Sequencing.**
5	She will breathe fire and make clouds.	Encourage the children to justify their prediction using the text, to check their understanding. If they do not mention breathing fire and bringing night-time like the other night dragons, prompt them to further their prediction to include them. **Award 1 mark for a plausible prediction.** **Skill: Prediction.**

The Night Dragon, by Naomi Howarth

This text is from *The Night Dragon*, which is the tale of a dragon called Maud who lives with four other dragons. Maud believes she isn't a night dragon, but does she just need to believe in herself?

On top of a very high mountain, in a land far away, lived a dragon. Her name was Maud. Maud was one of five dragons, but she wasn't like the others at all. They were night dragons.

Every evening, when the sun was low in the sky, Delbert, Gar, Brimlad and Nelda would wake up from a long sleep. They would swoop into the air, breathing huge flames of fire, and fill the sky with great grey, sooty clouds. As these clouds covered the sun, darkness would fall, and day would turn to night. But Maud didn't fly, breathe fire, or cast great grey, sooty clouds over the land.

"Why don't you fly, Maud?" snarled Delbert.

"She's a weedy wimp! Her wings are too weak," croaked Gar.

"She's not tough enough to take on the sun!" shouted Brimlad.

"It's best if she doesn't bother, the pretty little thing!" cackled Nelda.

"It must be true," thought Maud. "I'll never be a night dragon."

Maud's only friend was Mouse. "I wish I could fly, and breathe fire, and fill the sky with great grey, sooty clouds," Maud would say.

"But you could, Maud!" Mouse always squeaked. "Don't listen to the others! If you tried, you'd see that you can do those things just fine. You don't need to be a big, scary brute to be a night dragon. You just need to be yourself." But Maud didn't quite believe him.

One afternoon, on the day of Brimlad's 557th birthday, he decided to throw a party. All the dragons were invited, except for Maud. Maud watched as they ate, drank and fought until one by one, each dragon fell into a deep, unshakeable sleep.

As the day drew on, the dragons still didn't wake up. Maud looked out over the land, but something was very different. The sky was completely empty! There were no clouds, and nightfall was nowhere to be seen. Maud didn't know what to do.

"Maud," said Mouse, "you have to try and fly, otherwise the sky will stay light all night!"

"I can't!" whispered Maud. "I'm afraid to."

"I know you can do it, Maud," insisted Mouse. "I will come with you, and we can fly together."

With Mouse's words in her ear, Maud felt a little bit braver. There was only one thing for it ...

Maud stepped off the edge of the mountain, and began tumbling through the air. "Use your wings, Maud!" squeaked Mouse. Maud beat her wings as hard as she could and suddenly, the ground grew smaller. She wasn't tumbling any more. She was soaring!

Inference

Name: ____________________

1 Why do you think Maud didn't think she was a real night dragon?

____

____ 1 mark

2 How do you think the other dragons felt about Maud? Tick **one**.

She was a special dragon. ☐

She was not a real night dragon. ☐

She was the same as them. ☐

1 mark

3 Look at the paragraph beginning *As the day drew on ...* . Why was it a problem that all the night dragons were asleep?

____ 1 mark

4 *Maud stepped off the edge of the mountain, and began tumbling through the air.*
How do you think Maud felt at this point in the story?

____

____ 1 mark

5 At the end of the story, Maud was flying in the air. How do you think Mouse felt when he saw this? Tick **one**.

upset ☐

scared ☐

proud ☐

alone ☐

1 mark

Mix it up!

Name: ______________________

1 Look at the first paragraph. How many other dragons did Maud live with?

____

1 mark

2 How do you think Mouse felt when the other dragons were mean to Maud?

____

1 mark

3 *Maud watched as they ate, drank and fought until one by one, each dragon fell into a deep, unshakeable sleep.*
Which of these words could replace the word *watched* in this sentence? Tick **one**.

waited ☐

sang ☐

looked ☐

cried ☐

1 mark

4 Number the events to show the order in which they happened in the story. One has been done for you.

The other dragons called Maud names.	1
Maud flew in the air.	
The other dragons had a party.	
Maud stepped off the mountain.	

1 mark

5 At the end of the text, Maud was able to soar into the sky. What do you think will happen next in the story?

____

____

1 mark

How to Build a Gingerbread House

by Laura Lodge

Printable text • Modelling slides **Photocopiable text and questions • pages 104 to 107**

Baking is an activity that many children love to do, and what better to bake than your own gingerbread house? Some of the children may recognise the gingerbread house as a special Christmas tradition and others may recall that there is one in the traditional story of 'Hansel and Gretel'. In Units 11 and 12 we will explore two different versions of this traditional tale, so this is an ideal way to introduce the theme. You may wish to discuss the links between the three texts once the children have had the opportunity to read them all.

1 Get ready

Discuss the **Key vocabulary** identified in the **Language toolkit** and then complete the vocabulary and phonics activities as desired. Please note that the selected vocabulary is a guide. Depending on the needs of your cohort, additional vocabulary discussion may be beneficial before, during and after reading. Next, display the text (pages 104 to 105) so the children can see the title and any illustrations, and encourage the children to discuss the following questions before reading.

1. What type of text is this? How do you know?
   The children should be able to recognise this is a non-fiction text that gives the reader instructions. Answers here will depend on the children's prior exposure to this text type. You may wish to discuss when they have followed instructions before (e.g. lining up at playtime; following a recipe).

2. This text includes a recipe. What is a recipe? Have you ever followed one? If so, what for?
   Answers will vary depending on the children's exposure to recipes but they should be able to make a link between following a recipe and baking, based on work done at school. Some may also be able to contribute stories about following recipes at home.

3. The instructions in this text teach you how to make a gingerbread house. What is gingerbread? Have you ever eaten it or baked it?
   Answers will vary depending on the children's experiences. If they have never encountered gingerbread before, this may be a useful opportunity to give them some to try.

4. Have you ever seen a gingerbread house before? If so, where and when?
   Answers will vary depending on the children's experiences and previous exposure to fairy tales such as 'Hansel and Gretel'. You may wish to show some images of different gingerbread houses to support their understanding.

Language toolkit

Key vocabulary

decorating	delicious	equipment
illustration	ingredients	method

Vocabulary discussion questions

- When might you need to use **equipment** at school?
- Is an **illustration** the same as a drawing?
- Is tidying up the same as **decorating**?

Vocabulary activities

1. **Ingredients** uses the prefix 'in–' which means 'in' or 'into'. How many other words can the children find that start with 'in–'?
2. How many synonyms for **delicious** can the children find?

Phonics

–ment suffix	equipment
–ness suffix	thickness
Longer words	bicarbonate, carefully, chocolates, equipment, gingerbread, illustration, ingredients, instructions, whatever
Common exception words	find, sugar, water, would

Phonics activity

In pairs, ask the children to list other words they know that use the suffixes '–ment' and '–ness'. How many can they think of?

2 First steps

Read the text together and then encourage the children to discuss the following questions.

1 **Can you name four ingredients that you need to make the gingerbread house? What about four pieces of equipment?**
Answers will vary but encourage the children to look for the items in the ingredients and equipment lists (e.g. *butter, sugar, honey, flour/pan, mixing bowls, wooden spoons, paper*).

2 **Does the text say you should try to bake this on your own? Why? Why not?**
No, it tells us to ask an adult for help because we are going to be using a hot pan, an oven and scissors.

3 **What do you need to do first?**
Get our equipment and ingredients ready./Ask an adult to help us./Melt the first ingredients together.

4 **Did you like the text? Why? Why not?**
Answers will vary but encourage the children to explain their answers (e.g. *I liked it because I want to make my own gingerbread house*).

3 Explore

- Discuss the features of effective instructions. Why do instructions need to be clear, and use short sentences? Divide the children into pairs and give one of the pair a simple picture. Keeping the picture hidden, that child must explain to their partner how to draw it without showing it to them. Compare the drawings with the original pictures and discuss how the instructions affected the process.
- The author uses imperative verbs and command sentences to tell the reader what to do. Discuss what imperative verbs are, and the fact that they often come at the beginning of the sentence. Encourage the children to find as many as they can in the text.
- Emphasise that it is very important to keep safe when cooking. Discuss how they could do this (e.g. ask an adult to help when using the oven; make sure their work surface is tidy). You might ask if they, or their family, have ever had an accident in the kitchen. Discuss what we should and should not do to keep safe when cooking.

4 Skills focus

See pages 102 to 103

Use the information from the **Skills guide** and the relevant **Skills graphic** to introduce the skill of retrieval.

1 Model the skill using the **Unit 10 Modelling slides** and the **Modelling retrieval** guidance on page 102.

2 The children can then attempt the **Retrieval** questions on page 106.

3 Finally, the **Mix it up!** questions on page 107 offer practice in a range of comprehension skills.

Answers and marking guidance for all questions are included on pages 102 to 103.

5 Where next?

- Speaking and listening task: The children could work together to make safety videos that teach viewers how to stay safe while baking. The children could use the imperative verbs collected during the **Explore** session to command viewers into action.
- Writing task: The children could research different types of homes across the world (e.g. yurts in Mongolia; rondavels in Lesotho; cave homes in Tunisia). You could use some of the books in the **Reading list**. The children could create guides that give simple information about these different homes, comparing and contrasting their own homes with those in other countries.

Reading list

Fiction

- *Gingerbread Baby* by Jan Brett
- *The Gingerbread Girl* by Lisa Campbell Ernst
- *The Gingerbread Man 2: What Happened Later?* by Stephen Dixon
- *Hansel and Gretel* by Bethan Woollvin (Linked text: Unit 12)
- *Hansel and Gretel* by Laura Lodge (Linked text: Unit 11)

Class reads

- *The Gingerbread Man* by Gail Yerrill

Non-fiction

- *The Best Ever Baking Book* by Jane Bull
- *Children Like Us: Homes Around The World* by Moira Butterfield
- *Let's Build a House* by Mick Manning and Brita Granström
- *No-Bake Gingerbread Houses for Kids* by Lisa Turner Anderson

Poetry

- *Hooray for Bread* by Allan Ahlberg and Bruce Ingman

Modelling retrieval

See Unit 10 Modelling slides

Use the **Skills guide** (see pages 16 to 17) and the downloadable **Skills graphic** to support your modelling.

1 Look at the first paragraph of the text. Who lives in a gingerbread house?

the witch from 'Hansel and Gretel'

Read the question together and model using the locator to find the relevant paragraph. Then model identifying key words before scanning the first paragraph together. Some children may attempt to answer using their extrinsic knowledge or memory. In this case, remind them that we are retrieving information. Think aloud: *Can you put your finger on 'witch'?* Some children may answer with just 'a witch' but point out that the text tells us it is the witch from 'Hansel and Gretel'.

2 What should you add with the ginger? Tick two.

honey ☐ butter ☐ flour ☑ sugar ☐ allspice ☑

Read the question together and model identifying the key words and the expectation of 'Tick two'. This question does not have a locator so model scanning for the key words 'add' and 'ginger'. This is a tricky question as the distractors 'honey', 'butter' and 'sugar' are included in the same step of the recipe as the target sentence. Once you have found the correct sentence, model using 'Fastest finger first' (see page 17) to prove your answer. If the children struggle, encourage them to focus only on the sentence that contains 'ginger'.

3 Where should the gingerbread go after you roll it out?

on the baking tray

Read the question together and model identifying the key words (e.g. 'gingerbread', 'after', 'roll'). This question does not have a locator and therefore the key word 'roll' is important. Although this may seem like a simple question, it is likely that many children will respond with a reference to the oven, relying on memory rather than using the text. In this case, refocus them on the key word 'roll'. Think aloud: *What do we have to do next?* Continue by reading the next sentence and model finding the answer in the text.

4 What does the text warn you not to do? Tick one.

burn yourself ☐ mix too slowly ☐ press too hard ☑ cut yourself ☐

Read the question together and model identifying the key word 'warn'. Discuss the meaning of 'warn' and any synonyms that may be used (e.g. 'be careful'). The distractors in this question are tricky as they could all be inferred as warnings, especially the first option, given the many references to the need for adult help. Explain that, as we are retrieving information, we must use 'Fastest finger first' to locate a warning in the text.

Retrieval questions mark scheme

See page 106

Answer	Guidance
1 plain *OR* plain flour	Some children may find this challenging as there is no locator and the answer is within the Ingredients section. In this case, remind them to read the whole text, not only the method. **Award 1 mark for a correct answer.**
2 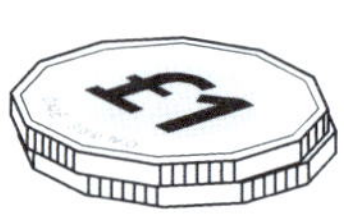 ☑	This is an unusual question as it requires the children to retrieve information and translate this into an image. If they find this tricky, attempt some other questions that follow a similar format, modelling the best way to answer them. **Award 1 mark for the correct answer ticked.**
3 warm water	Some children may only respond with 'water'. In this case, remind them that the question provides the clue 'find and copy two words'. **Award 1 mark for the correct answer.**

Answer	Guidance
4 decorate the house	Some children may use their extrinsic knowledge here and give a response such as 'eat them'. In this case, it is important to remind them to use the text and 'Fastest finger first' (see page 17) to ensure they reach an appropriate answer. **Award 1 mark for any reference to decorating the house.**
5 paper – draw out shapes rolling pin – roll out gingerbread pan – melt ingredients	This question requires understanding of the whole text. Some children may benefit from being reminded to match the statements they are certain of first, leaving the statement they are finding most challenging until last. **Award 1 mark for all pairs correctly matched.**

Mix it up! questions mark scheme

See page 107

Answer	Guidance
1 to make sure we don't have an accident/ cut ourselves	Some children may answer vaguely, referring to it always being the case (e.g. 'we always have an adult with us'). If so, encourage them to extend their response with an example (e.g. 'we always have to have an adult help us because the oven is dangerous'). **Award 1 mark for any plausible reference to keeping safe. Also accept a specific reference to a possible injury or danger.** Skill: Inference.
2 sugar and honey	Some children may only provide one ingredient. In this case, hint that there are two parts to the answer. Refocus them on the target sentence and ask them to check that they have answered the question fully using all the information in the text. **Award 1 mark for both 'sugar' and 'honey' being written (in any order).** Skill: Retrieval.
3 pieces	Some children may answer 'shapes'. This should be accepted but it would be useful to clarify with them why 'pieces' is a more appropriate response (e.g. 'parts' and 'pieces' can be of anything but 'shapes' are a very specific thing). **Award 1 mark for the correct answer.** Skill: Word meaning.
4 You might burn yourself. ✓	This is a prediction question in an unusual format. The children may benefit from you explaining that it is a prediction question and that they will need to use their inference skills to answer it. Encourage them to justify their prediction using the text to check their understanding. **Award 1 mark for the correct answer ticked.** Skill: Prediction.
5 Melt the butter. ✓	If the children find this sequencing question challenging, encourage them to use a highlighter to locate the statements within the text. This will then support them to find the first statement. **Award 1 mark for the correct answer ticked.** Skill: Sequencing.

How to Build a Gingerbread House, by Laura Lodge

This text is a set of instructions on how to bake and build your own gingerbread house. Baking is fun, but make sure you always ask an adult to help you.

There is a famous traditional tale called 'Hansel and Gretel', where a witch lives inside a house made from delicious gingerbread. Would you like to make your own gingerbread house like the one in the illustration? Follow these instructions with an adult to find out how!

Ingredients

For the gingerbread:

250g unsalted butter

200g dark brown sugar

7tbsp honey

600g plain flour

2tsp bicarbonate of soda

4tsp ground ginger

2tsp allspice

For decorating:

500g icing sugar

warm water

small sweets or chocolates

Equipment

pan

mixing bowls

wooden spoons

paper

pencil

scissors

rolling pin

baking tray

knife

Method

1. First, ask an adult to help you make the gingerbread by melting the butter, sugar and honey together in a pan. Mix together the flour, bicarbonate of soda, ginger and allspice in a mixing bowl. Then add the butter mixture and mix well.

2. Decide what shape you would like your gingerbread house to be. You will need six pieces: two side walls, a front and a back wall, and two pieces for the roof. You might like to use the same shapes as are given below. Ask an adult to help you carefully measure and draw out the shapes on some paper. Then cut them out.

3. Roll out your gingerbread until it is the same thickness as two £1 coins. Put the gingerbread on the baking tray. Then use your paper shapes to cut out the sections you need. Ask an adult to help you.

4. Bake your gingerbread in the oven at 180 degrees for 12 to 15 minutes. Then ask an adult to help you take it out and leave it to cool.

5. Mix the icing sugar with warm water until it becomes thick icing. Use this to stick your gingerbread together into the shape of a house. Be careful not to press too hard.

6. Use the rest of the icing to decorate your house using sweets, chocolates or whatever you like.

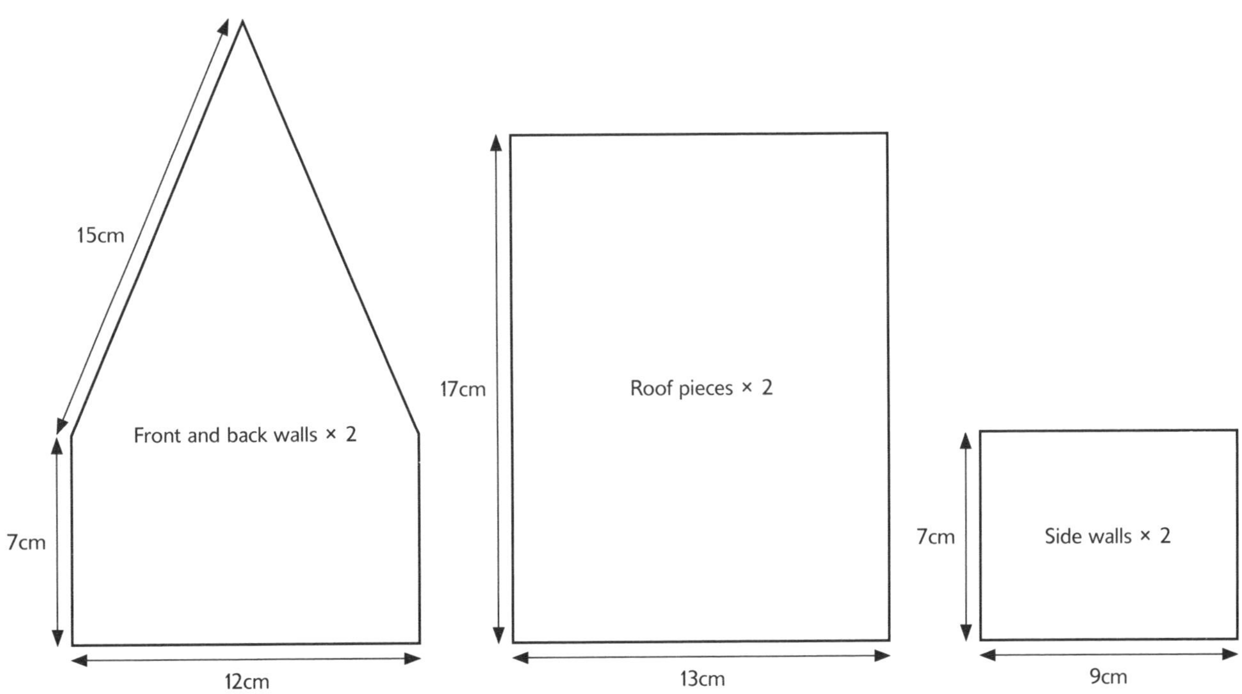

Retrieval

Name: ______________________

1 What type of flour do you need to use?

______________________ 1 mark

2 According to the text, how thick should the gingerbread be?
Tick the best picture.

☐

☐

☐

☐

1 mark

3 Look at step 5. Find and copy **two** words that tell you what to mix with the icing sugar.

______________________ 1 mark

4 What should you do with the sweets?

____

______________________ 1 mark

5 Draw lines to show what each piece of equipment is used for.

paper	roll out gingerbread
rolling pin	melt ingredients
pan	draw out shapes

1 mark

Mix it up!

Name: ______________________________

1 Why do you think the text tells you to ask an adult for help?

____

____ 1 mark

2 What should you melt with the butter?

____ 1 mark

3 Look at step 2. Find and copy **one** word that means the same as 'parts'.

______________________________ 1 mark

4 Look at step 4. What could happen if you started to build the house without leaving the gingerbread to cool? Tick **one**.

It might melt. ☐

You might burn it. ☐

You might burn yourself. ☐

Nothing. ☐

1 mark

5 Which instruction comes first in the text? Tick **one**.

Cut the gingerbread. ☐

Melt the butter. ☐

Add the allspice. ☐

Roll out the gingerbread. ☐

1 mark

Unit 11

Retrieval

Fiction

Hansel and Gretel

by Laura Lodge

Printable text • Modelling slides   Photocopiable text and questions • pages 112 to 115

Children love this fairy tale, especially hearing about the witch's gingerbread house, covered in sweets and icing. You may wish to make links back to the instructional text in Unit 10. In this traditional version of the story, we follow the siblings Hansel and Gretel on their journey through the forest. This text is the first of two focusing on Hansel and Gretel: Unit 12 is an extract from Bethan Woollvin's topsy-turvy retelling.

1 Get ready

Discuss the **Key vocabulary** identified in the **Language toolkit** and then complete the vocabulary and phonics activities as desired. Please note that the selected vocabulary is a guide. Depending on the needs of your cohort, additional vocabulary discussion may be beneficial before, during and after reading. Next, display the text (pages 112 to 113) so the children can see the title and any illustrations, and encourage the children to discuss the following questions before reading.

1 This story is a traditional tale or fairy tale. A traditional tale is an old story that people have been telling for many years, so that lots of different versions exist. What other traditional tales can you name?
The children should be able to contribute a number of traditional tales they have encountered during their time at school. If possible, encourage discussion of traditional tales from other cultures.

2 One of the characters in this text is a witch. What is a witch?
Answers will vary depending on the children's exposure to texts but all should be able to explain that witches use magic. Many children will be aware of traditionally negative portrayals of witches.

3 We have talked about heroes and villains before (see Unit 8, *Sir Charlie Stinky Socks*). Do you think heroes are *always* good and villains are *always* bad?
Answers will vary depending on the texts the children have encountered. However, it is likely that they will answer 'yes'. Explain that Hansel and Gretel are the heroes in this story, but we will see that they sometimes need to do bad things.

4 This story also features an evil stepmother. Can you think of any other stories with an evil stepmother?
Answers will vary depending on the children's exposure to texts but are likely to include some reference to Cinderella.

Language toolkit

Key vocabulary

ancient	cackled	demanded
exclaimed	fooled	instead
shrieked	stepmother	

Vocabulary discussion questions

- When you **exclaim** something, are you speaking loudly or quietly?
- What is the difference between something that is old and something that is **ancient**?
- Have you ever been **fooled** by someone? How?

Vocabulary activities

1 Ask the children to experiment with talking in different ways based on the text. They could try **exclaiming**, **shrieking** and **cackling**.

2 How many synonyms for **ancient** can the children find? What about words meaning the opposite?

Phonics

-ly suffix	happily, luckily, politely, tightly, unfortunately
Longer words	decided, demanded, gingerbread, happily, luckily, politely, stepmother, terrible, unfortunately
Common exception words	after, any, beautiful, break, children, climb(ed), could, door, every, father, find, hold, kind, old, told, water, who

Phonics activity

How many common exception words can the children find? Can they use one to add an extra sentence to the story?

2 First steps

Read the text together and then encourage the children to discuss the following questions.

1 **Where is the story set? Do we know which country it is set in?**
In/near a forest/wood. The children may guess a country using the details in the text and the illustration. Explain to them that the traditional tale is set in Germany, and that Hansel and Gretel are German names.

2 **There are five characters in this story. Can you name all of them?**
Stepmother, father, Hansel, Gretel and the witch.

3 **What does Hansel and Gretel's stepmother try to do at the start of the story?**
She tries to get rid of her stepchildren by leaving them in the forest.

4 **Did you like the text? Why? Why not?**
Answers will vary but encourage the children to explain their answers (e.g. *I liked it because Hansel and Gretel manage to get rid of the witch and they live happily ever after*).

3 Explore

- Discuss what the children should do if they ever get lost. Ask them how they can keep safe and find their way back to somewhere they know. Discuss strategies they could use if this happens, such as finding a police officer or going to a shop and asking for help.
- Discuss whether the children have ever had to look after a sister, brother or friend in a difficult situation. What did they do? How did they help to keep themselves and their friend safe? Would they do anything differently if it happened again?
- In fairy tales such as 'Hansel and Gretel', many characters trick each other (e.g. the stepmother tricks the father in 'Hansel and Gretel'; the wolf tricks Little Red Riding Hood). Encourage the children to discuss other examples of trickery that they can recall from the text and fairy tales in general.
- The author uses different adjectives to describe the characters. How many different character adjectives can the children find? They could go on a synonym hunt to find different ways to describe each character.

4 Skills focus

See pages 110 to 111

Use the information from the **Skills guide** and the relevant **Skills graphic** to introduce the skill of retrieval.

1 Model the skill using the **Unit 11 Modelling slides** and the **Modelling retrieval** guidance on page 110.

2 The children can then attempt the **Retrieval** questions on page 114.

3 Finally, the **Mix it up!** questions on page 115 offer practice in a range of comprehension skills.

Answers and marking guidance for all questions are included on pages 110 to 111.

5 Where next?

- Speaking and listening task: Work together in groups to create gingerbread houses using a range of edible materials. The children could then work together to present their house to the class, 'selling' their houses to the highest bidder in a role-play property auction.
- Writing task: The children could create a 'wanted' poster that describes the evil stepmother as wanted for 'child desertion'. They could use vocabulary gathered in the synonym hunt during the **Explore** section to support them when describing the stepmother's appearance and character.

Reading list

Fiction

- *The Great Fairy Tale Disaster* by David Conway
- *Hansel and Gretel* by Bethan Woollvin (Linked text: Unit 12)
- *Inside the Villains* by Clotilde Perrin
- *The Jolly Postman* by Allan Ahlberg
- *Once Upon a Wild Wood* by Chris Riddell

Class reads

- *Hansel and Gretel* by Rachel Isadora

Non-fiction

- *Go Wild in the Woods* by Goldie Hawk
- *How to Build a Gingerbread House* by Laura Lodge (Linked text: Unit 10)
- *Nadiya's Bake Me a Story* by Nadiya Hussain

Poetry

- *Hansel and Gretel: A Favorite Story in Rhythm and Rhyme* by Nadia Higgins

Films

- *Hansel and Gretel* (Golan-Globus Productions, 1987)

Modelling retrieval

See Unit 11 Modelling slides

Use the **Skills guide** (see pages 16 to 17) and the downloadable **Skills graphic** to support your modelling.

1 **Look at the first paragraph. When did the children notice they were all alone?**

When it was getting dark.

Read the question together and model using the locator to find the relevant paragraph. Next, model identifying the key words before scanning the first paragraph for them together. Some children may use their inference skills and say 'evening' or similar. If so, remind them that they are retrieving information and ask them to put their finger on 'evening'.

2 ***After a few minutes, they came upon a house …* . What was the house made of? Tick two.**

icing ☑ biscuits ☐ gingerbread ☑ sprinkles ☐ sugar ☐

Read the question together. Model using the locator and identifying the key words and the expectation of 'Tick two'. Once you have found the correct sentence, model using 'Fastest finger first' (see page 17) to prove your answer. Some children may choose 'biscuits' or 'sugar'. Although these are both technically correct, remind them that as we are retrieving, we must take information straight from the text. To demonstrate this, ask them to scan for the word 'biscuits' – can they find it?

3 **How did the witch test whether Hansel was ready for cooking?**

She grabbed his finger.

Read the question together. This question does not have a locator and there is an added level of challenge as the key word in the question does not mirror that of the text ('test' rather than 'checked'). As part of your modelling, explain to the children that sometimes questions use synonyms, so we must always think through different ways to say the key words before scanning the text. Continue by discussing the fact that 'checked' is a synonym of 'test' and model finding it in the text to locate the answer.

4 **What happened to the witch at the end of the story?**

The witch climbed into the oven.

Read the question together and model locating the last section of the story that includes the witch. This question is a simple retrieval exercise; however, many children may be tempted to use inference (e.g. the witch was cooked/killed in the oven by Gretel). If so, encourage them to use 'Fastest finger first' to prove their retrieval as the text merely says that the witch climbed into the oven, the door was shut and that was the end of the witch.

Retrieval questions mark scheme

See page 114

Answer	Guidance
1 She pretended to be a kind lady.	Some children may use a vague response such as 'she tricked them'. Although this is technically correct, ask the children for more detail to ensure they have understood the question before awarding the mark. Encourage them to use words and phrases from the text. **Award 1 mark for any reference to the witch pretending to be kind or help them.**
2 She wanted to fatten him up.	Some children may benefit from having a locator (fifth paragraph) to support them here. If the children respond with other events (e.g. 'throw him into a cage') ask them to reread the paragraph and discuss the difference between wanting to do something (fattening him up) and actually doing it (throwing him into the cage). **Award 1 mark for any reference to fattening him up.**

Answer		Guidance
3	She gave Hansel a bone to hold.	Some children may respond with 'Gretel tricked the witch into climbing into the oven'. As this is from the seventh paragraph it should not be accepted as correct. Remind the children to use any locators in the question to help them. **Award 1 mark for any reference to giving Hansel a bone to hold.**
4	Check the oven. ☑ Boil some water. ☑	Some children may choose 'Cook Hansel'. The witch is going to cook Hansel, and Gretel is asked to boil water for this, but Gretel is not ordered to cook him. If this option is chosen, refocus the children on the sentences beginning 'But one day …' and 'Hansel was about …'. Discuss the orders the witch actually gives. **Award 1 mark for the correct answers ticked.**
5	Hansel, Gretel and their father	Some children may include the witch or the stepmother in addition to Hansel, Gretel and their father. In this case, do not award 1 mark. Ask the children to check what the text says carefully, using 'Fastest finger first' (see page 17) to prove their responses. **Award 1 mark for referring to Hansel, Gretel and their father.**

Mix it up! questions mark scheme

See page 115

Answer		Guidance
1	She disliked them./She wanted their father to herself./She didn't want to have to look after them.	Some children may benefit from discussing this in pairs or small groups to gather ideas. All should be able to make a reference to her dislike of the children; however, many could be supported to extend this through questions and prompts. **Award 1 mark for any plausible reference to disliking them or not wanting to look after them.** **Skill: Inference.**
2	a part of the forest they had never been in before	Some children may provide a vague response that only refers to the forest/wood. If so, add the word 'exactly' to the question. Think aloud: *Where exactly did their stepmother leave Hansel and Gretel?* **Award 1 mark for any reference to a part of the forest they had never been in before.** **Skill: Retrieval.**
3	(chew)	Support the children to use the locator if needed. Remind them of the strategies we use for definition, such as substitution. Some may choose 'gobble'. If so, ask them to act out nibbling something, then gobbling something. Discuss the similarities and differences between the two – which other option is closer to the meaning of nibble? **Award 1 mark for the correct answer circled.** **Skill: Word meaning.**
4	Gretel planned their escape. ☑	The children need to understand the whole story to respond correctly here. If they find this question challenging, remind them to scan the text for key words from each statement and highlight them. This will support them to work out the correct order. **Award 1 mark for the correct answer ticked.** **Skill: Sequencing.**
5	She would run away to another forest and build another gingerbread house so that she could find other children to eat.	Encourage the children to justify their prediction using the text to check their understanding. **Award 1 mark for a plausible prediction.** **Skill: Prediction.**

Hansel and Gretel, by Laura Lodge

This text is a version of a well-known traditional tale. Two children, Hansel and Gretel, are left alone in the forest by their evil stepmother. Will they get back home safely?

Once upon a time, two children lived with their father and stepmother at the edge of a large forest. One day, the family went for a walk deep in the beautiful wood. While Hansel and Gretel played, their evil stepmother tricked their father into leaving them in the wood. It was getting dark by the time the children noticed they were all alone. Luckily, the day before had been rainy so they could follow their father's footsteps all the way home.

"Oh children, we were so worried!" exclaimed their stepmother, as their father hugged Hansel and Gretel tightly.

The next day, the terrible stepmother politely asked the children to help her collect some wood. Once they were in a part of the forest the children had never been in before, the horrible stepmother left them all alone. The children were scared but they started trying to get back home. After a few minutes, they came upon a house made of gingerbread, with a roof covered in icing and windows made out of sweets. Hansel and Gretel were hungry, so they began to break off bits of the house to eat.

"Who dares to nibble my house?" shrieked an angry voice from inside. Hansel and Gretel felt terrible and said sorry to the ancient woman who wandered out of the house. When the children told the lady all about their evil stepmother, she said, "Well, come and live with me, my dears. I will take care of you." Unfortunately, the old woman was not really kind – she was a witch and she planned to eat Hansel and Gretel. Once the children were tucked up in bed, feeling safe, she cackled, "They won't escape now!" and laughed an evil laugh.

As soon as the children woke up in the morning, the witch grabbed Hansel and dragged him to the kitchen. Throwing him into a small cage, she giggled and said, “You'll be delicious once I've fattened you up!” First Gretel sobbed but then she stopped crying and started to plan their escape.

The witch was blind and checked Hansel every morning by grabbing his finger to feel if it was fatter. Gretel gave her brother a bone to hold instead, which fooled the wicked witch for weeks. But one day the witch decided that she could not wait any longer and ordered Gretel to boil some water. Hansel was about to be cooked.

While the water was boiling, the witch demanded that Gretel check the oven but Gretel was too clever for her. “I don't know how,” Gretel told the witch. The witch climbed into the oven to show her how. BANG! Gretel slammed the oven door shut. That was the end of the wicked witch.

“Hansel! Gretel! Where are you?” shouted a voice. It was their father, who had come to find them. Hansel, Gretel and their father lived happily ever after in the gingerbread house.

Retrieval

Name: ______________________

1 Look at the fourth paragraph. How did the witch make Hansel and Gretel go into her house?

____

____ 1 mark

2 What did the witch want to do to Hansel before she cooked him?

____

____ 1 mark

3 Look at the sixth paragraph. How did Gretel fool the witch?

____

____ 1 mark

4 Look at the section beginning *The witch was blind* ... to the end of the story. What did the witch order Gretel to do? Tick **two**.

Cook Hansel. ☐

Check the oven. ☐

Make lunch. ☐

Boil some water. ☐

1 mark

5 Who lived in the gingerbread house at the end of the story?

____

____ 1 mark

Mix it up!

Name: ____________________

1 Why do you think the stepmother wanted to leave the children in the forest?

____

____

______________________________ 1 mark

2 Look at the third paragraph. Where did their stepmother leave Hansel and Gretel?

______________________________ 1 mark

3 Look at the sentence beginning *"Who dares to nibble my house?"*. Which of these words could replace the word *nibble* in this sentence? Circle **one**.

gobble | giggle | look | chew

1 mark

4 Which of these events happened first? Tick **one**.

Gretel boiled some water.	☐
Gretel gave Hansel a bone.	☐
Gretel slammed the oven door shut.	☐
Gretel planned their escape.	☐

1 mark

5 Imagine that the witch escaped. What do you think she would do next?

____

____

______________________________ 1 mark

Hansel and Gretel

by Bethan Woollvin

Printable text • Modelling slides   Photocopiable text and questions • pages 120 to 123

This version of 'Hansel and Gretel' turns the story upside down. If Unit 11 has been completed, encourage the children to compare the two texts.

1 Get ready

Discuss the **Key vocabulary** identified in the **Language toolkit** and then complete the vocabulary and phonics activities as desired. Please note that the selected vocabulary is a guide. Depending on the needs of your cohort, additional vocabulary discussion may be beneficial before, during and after reading. Next, display the text (pages 120 to 121) so the children can see the title and any illustrations, and encourage the children to discuss the following questions before reading.

1 This story is another version of 'Hansel and Gretel'. Can you retell the traditional story?
The children should all be able to retell the traditional story (as told in Unit 11).

2 Sometimes traditional tales can be retold in different ways. Can you think of another fairy tale that has been mixed up?
Answers will vary depending on the children's exposure to texts and the children may need some prompting (e.g. *The Wolf's Story* based on 'Little Red Riding Hood').

3 What do you think might be different about this version of 'Hansel and Gretel'?
Answers will vary but the important point is that the children join in with the discussion and justify their opinions.

4 Are witches always evil characters? Can you think of any books where they are **not** the villains?
Answers will vary depending on the children's exposure to texts but all should be able to contribute an opinion. The children may refer to the *Harry Potter* books or *The Worst Witch*.

Language toolkit

Key vocabulary

collapsed	couldn't believe her eyes	entirely
made themselves at home	magic	trail

Vocabulary discussion questions

- Do you think it would be easier to learn if your classroom was **entirely** made of sweets?
- Have you ever followed a **trail**?
- Which is more likely to **collapse**: a chair with one person on or a chair with five people on?

Vocabulary activities

1 Discuss the phrases **couldn't believe her eyes** and **made themselves at home**. Ask the children to 'put their thinking caps on' and think of some other idioms.

2 Use one of the vocabulary activities on page 15 to investigate some of the key words above.

Phonics

–ful suffix	careful, mouthful
Contracted forms	didn't, don't, I'm, it's, wasn't, we're
Longer words	decided, delicious, demanded, gingerbread, unluckily
Common exception words	after, because, children, could(n't), even, eye(s), most, only, who, would

Phonics activity

How many words can the children find with the suffixes '–ed', '–ly', '–ing' and '–ful'?

2 First steps

Read the text together and then encourage the children to discuss the following questions.

1 **Does this version of 'Hansel and Gretel' have a different setting from the one you already know? Are the characters the same?**
The setting is similar – in a wood/forest. The characters of Hansel, Gretel and the witch appear but the stepmother and father do not. Both of the witches live in gingerbread houses.

2 **What is different about the events in this version of the story?**
Answers will vary but are likely to focus on Willow being a good witch; Hansel and Gretel being naughty; Willow trying to be kind to Hansel and Gretel; and the ending.

3 **In this version, who are the heroes and who are the villains? Why?**
Willow the witch is the hero because she is kind to Hansel and Gretel. Hansel and Gretel are the villains because they eat Willow's house and make a mess.

4 **Did you like the text? Why? Why not?**
Answers will vary but encourage the children to explain their answers (e.g. *I liked Willow because she is a good witch but I thought the children were very mean to her*).

3 Explore

- Willow is a good witch who tries to look after Hansel and Gretel by inviting them into her home and cooking them food because they are hungry and alone. Discuss how the children can help people in need.
- Willow tries to do the right thing even when Hansel and Gretel are mean to her. Discuss times when the children have 'done the right thing' and 'risen above' something even though they didn't want to.
- The author repeats the phrase 'Willow was a good witch'. Ask the children why they think she does that. What effect does it have on us as the readers? At the end, this is contrasted with the phrase 'Willow was not ALWAYS a good witch'. Ask the children why they think the author changed the sentence there.

4 Skills focus

See pages 118 to 119

Use the information from the **Skills guide** and the relevant **Skills graphic** to introduce the skill of inference.

1 Model the skill using the **Unit 12 Modelling slides** and the **Modelling inference** guidance on page 118.

2 The children can then attempt the **Inference** questions on page 122.

3 Finally, the **Mix it up!** questions on page 123 offer practice in a range of comprehension skills.

Answers and marking guidance for all questions are included on pages 118 to 119.

5 Where next?

- Speaking and listening task: Working in groups, the children could use words and actions to dramatise the story of 'Hansel and Gretel'. They could retell different versions of the story, including the traditional story from Unit 11, this version and any other versions they can find. They could even retell the story from a particular character's point of view.
- Writing task: The children could work together to write their own mixed-up fairy tale or alternative narrative from a choice of lesser known traditional tales (e.g. 'The Elves and the Shoemaker', 'Rumpelstiltskin' or 'The Emperor's New Clothes'). The children could illustrate their stories or even create dioramas to support retelling their tale.

Reading list

Fiction

- *Hans Christian Andersen's Fairy Tales* by Hans Christian Andersen
- *Hansel and Gretel* by Bethan Woollvin
- *Hansel and Gretel* by Laura Lodge (Linked text: Unit 11)
- *Hansel and Gretel* by Michael Morpurgo
- *Mixed Up Fairy Tales* by Hilary Robinson
- *Rapunzel* by Bethan Woollvin
- *Trust Me, Hansel and Gretel Are Sweet!* by Nancy Loewen

Class reads

- *Fairy Tales from the Brothers Grimm* by the Brothers Grimm

Non-fiction

- *How to Build a Gingerbread House* by Laura Lodge (Linked text: Unit 10)
- *The Woodland Book* by Emily Bone and Alice James

Poetry

- *Firecrackers* by Zaro Weil
- *Revolting Rhymes* by Roald Dahl

Play

- *Fairy Tale Play* by Julia Spiers

Modelling inference

See Unit 12 Modelling slides

Use the **Skills guide** (see pages 20 to 21) and the downloadable **Skills graphic** to support your modelling.

1 How were other witches different to Willow?

They were bad and used bad magic.

Read the question together. There is no locator in this question, so model finding the key words and thinking of synonyms to support scanning the text (e.g. synonyms for 'different' could be 'wasn't like' or 'not like'). Once you have found the appropriate sentence, model 'what we know' (that Willow is a good witch who does good magic; that she is not like other witches) and from that, 'what we think'. Some children may retrieve 'she was a good witch' and 'only used good magic'; however, this does not answer the question. Explain that those phrases are about Willow and the question is asking about the other witches. If the children respond with 'they were bad', encourage them to expand their answer to discuss the 'bad magic' other witches used.

2 Look at the second paragraph. How do you think Willow felt when Hansel and Gretel left her to tidy up on her own?

frustrated/upset/annoyed/hurt

Read the question together and model using the locator and identifying the key words. Next, model saying 'what we know' (the children make a mess, Willow asks for help and they leave her to clean up their mess alone) and from that, make inferences together for 'what we think'. Some children may respond that she felt 'angry'. If so, reread the final sentence of that paragraph. Think aloud: *The text tells us she did not get angry so we need an emotion that is less severe than that, such as annoyed.* Discuss the children's ideas together.

3 Do you think Hansel and Gretel felt bad about eating Willow's house? Explain why.

No – because they ignored her when she asked them to stop and just said "But it's so tasty!". They never said sorry.

Read the question together. This question does not have a locator so needs careful modelling using the 'what we know' and 'what we think' structure as used in **Modelling questions 1** and **2** above. Some children may become confused between this and the traditional story, as the children in that version do apologise. If so, reread the relevant parts of this unit's text together and scan for the word 'sorry'. The word is not there so continue by discussing whether the children think Hansel and Gretel feel bad or not.

4 *But this time Willow did get angry. Because Willow was not ALWAYS a good witch.* What do you think Willow did at the end of the text?

Willow put a spell on Hansel and Gretel so that they could not move and cause more trouble.

Read the question together and model locating the last section of the text. This question can be answered in various ways depending on the children's ideas. As part of your modelling, ask them to think of different scenarios in groups, linking their ideas to the text. There is no incorrect response here as long as the children use the text to infer that Willow might do something to punish Hansel and Gretel. In the book, the story ends with Willow turning Hansel and Gretel into gingerbread biscuits. Share the final image from the book or explain the ending to the children.

Inference questions mark scheme

See page 122

	Answer	Guidance
1	People are scared of witches./She didn't want people to know she was a witch./She didn't want people to eat her house.	Some children may provide a vague response such as 'she wanted to'. In this case, work with them to think of reasons connected to the text. **Award 1 mark for a plausible reason.**
2	They were eating her house. *OR* They ate all the food.	Some children may respond with reasons from earlier or later in the text. In this case, remind them to use the locator and discuss whether their inference comes from the third paragraph or another paragraph. **Award 1 mark for a correct answer.**

Answer		Guidance
3	upset	Some children may use weaker synonyms such as 'sad'. Accept this answer but encourage them to work in a group to investigate a wider range of synonyms. **Award 1 mark for any reference to a plausible emotion.**
4	So they could do whatever they wanted. ☑	Some children may choose 'So they could eat it.' If so, refocus them on what we know from earlier in the story. Think aloud: *What have Hansel and Gretel done already? They have already been eating the house so they do not need to get rid of Willow to eat it.* **Award 1 mark for the correct answer ticked.**
5	upset because they realised how mean they had been	Some children may give a reason that is not connected to the text (e.g. they were hungry). This should not be accepted as it does not show understanding of the correct part of the text. **Award 1 mark for any reference to a plausible emotion. Award another 1 mark for an appropriate reason for the emotion.**

Mix it up! questions mark scheme

See page 123

Answer		Guidance
1	birds ☑ mice ☑	Some children may need reminding that this is a retrieval question and that they should therefore use 'Fastest finger first' (see page 17) to find the correct answer. **Award 1 mark for the correct answers ticked.** Skill: Retrieval.
2	delicious ☑	Some children may choose 'sugary' as the gingerbread will be sugary; however, this is incorrect. In this case, remind them that we are looking for the word closest in meaning to 'tasty' and discuss whether all sugary things are tasty. **Award 1 mark for the correct answer ticked.** Skill: Word meaning.
3	Gretel pushed Willow into the oven.	Some children may benefit from having a locator (e.g. in the last paragraph) to support them with this question. Some may read on further. If so, refocus them on the wording of the question 'straight after'. **Award 1 mark for any reference to Willow being pushed in the oven.** Skill: Sequencing.
4	upset/devastated	Some children may answer with the word 'angry'. This is technically correct; however, as it is directly in the text it should not be accepted, as this is an inference question. In this case, ask the children to use their inference skills to choose another emotion. **Award 1 mark for any reference to a plausible emotion.** Skill: Inference.
5	She will rebuild her house and put special spells on it to protect it from naughty children.	Encourage the children to justify their prediction using the text to check their understanding. **Award 1 mark for a plausible prediction.** Skill: Prediction.

Hansel and Gretel, by Bethan Woollvin

This text is from a story that tells a different version of the traditional tale of 'Hansel and Gretel'. In this text, Willow the good witch tries to look after Hansel and Gretel. Will she always be good?

Deep in the forest lived a witch named Willow. Willow wasn't like most witches. She was a good witch, who only used good magic. Willow had even made herself a home – entirely out of gingerbread.

One day while out in the forest, Willow spotted a trail of breadcrumbs which she decided to follow. At the end of the trail, she found two children. "We're Hansel and Gretel. What do you want?" demanded the children. "I'm worried these breadcrumbs might lead birds and mice to my gingerbread home," said Willow. "Please could you help me clean them up?" Hansel and Gretel didn't like this idea, so they left Willow to tidy up on her own. But Willow did not get angry, because Willow was a good witch.

When she arrived home, Willow couldn't believe her eyes. "Hansel, Gretel, please don't eat my house!" Willow cried. "But it's so tasty!" Gretel said, with a mouthful of gingerbread. Hansel and Gretel must be very hungry, Willow thought to herself. So she invited them in for dinner. While Hansel and Gretel made themselves at home, Willow used her best and most delicious spells to cook up a feast for them all. Unluckily for Willow, when she got to the table she found that Hansel and Gretel had already gobbled up all of the food! But Willow did not get angry, because Willow was a good witch.

It wasn't long before Willow had more to worry about than her rumbling tummy. Hansel and Gretel had found Willow's spells and wands, and began to play with them. "Please be careful with my magic things!"

Willow cried. But Hansel and Gretel still would not listen. The magic grew and grew and … grew!

Wanting the house all to themselves, Hansel and Gretel agreed to get rid of Willow. Gretel pushed the witch into the oven and the naughty twins carried on filling her home with spells … until it was bursting with magic! It wasn't long before Willow's home collapsed. It was only made out of gingerbread, after all. But this time Willow did get angry. Because Willow was not ALWAYS a good witch.

Inference

Name: ______________________

1 *Deep in the forest lived a witch named Willow.*
Why do you think Willow lived in the forest?

____

____ 1 mark

2 Look at the third paragraph. Give one reason why Willow might not have liked Hansel and Gretel.

____

____ 1 mark

3 *"Please be careful with my magic things!" Willow cried.*
How do you think Willow was feeling at this point in the story?

____ 1 mark

4 Look at the last paragraph. Why do you think Hansel and Gretel wanted the house all to themselves? Tick **one**.

So they could eat it. ☐

So they could clean it up. ☐

So they could do whatever they wanted. ☐

So they could cook Willow. ☐

1 mark

5 How do you think Hansel and Gretel felt when Willow's house collapsed?

____

Why?

____

____ 2 marks

Mix it up!

Name: ____________________

1 Look at the second paragraph. Willow was worried about the breadcrumbs. What creatures did she think the breadcrumbs would lead to her house? Tick **two**.

children ☐

birds ☐

cats ☐

mice ☐

1 mark

2 *"But it's so tasty!" Gretel said, with a mouthful of gingerbread.* Which of these words could replace *tasty*? Tick **one**.

salty ☐

sugary ☐

delicious ☐

dangerous ☐

1 mark

3 What happened straight after Hansel and Gretel agreed to get rid of Willow?

____

____

1 mark

4 Look at the last paragraph. How do you think Willow felt when her home collapsed?

____

1 mark

5 What do you think Willow will do when Hansel and Gretel have gone?

____

____

____

1 mark

The Life of Roald Dahl: A Marvellous Adventure by Emma Fischel

Printable text   Photocopiable text and questions • pages 125 to 127

This text is a simple biography of the much-loved author. It focuses on Dahl's childhood, recounting his time at school; his summer holidays in Norway; and his first job in East Africa. It is written in a story-like style that shares some of Dahl's trademark humour. Point out to the children that this text is about the life of the author of the next text, *George's Marvellous Medicine* (Unit 13). After reading both texts, you may wish to explore the links between them and discuss some of Roald Dahl's other books, such as *The Minpins* and *Matilda*. **For guidance on running this task, see page 11.**

Progress check questions mark scheme

Answer	Guidance
1 famous	Some children may need to be reminded to look for key words in the question; in 'find and copy' questions it is particularly important to check how many words the question is asking for. (In Progress check 3, answers containing more than one word will no longer be awarded marks.) **Award 1 mark for the correct answer. Also accept 'most famous' but address this misconception.** **Skill: Word meaning.**
2 cars ✓ sweet shops ✓	Some children may not tick 'cars' because the text says that there 'weren't many' cars. If so, talk about the meaning of that sentence. Think aloud: *Does it mean there weren't **any** cars?* **Award 1 mark for the correct answers ticked.** **Skill: Retrieval.**
3 He felt excited because there was lots to see.	Most children will respond with a positive emotion such as 'happy' or 'excited'. However, answers referring to negative feelings should also be accepted if they make reference to the text. Some children may struggle to justify their response. In this case, encourage them to put themselves in Roald's shoes – how would they feel? Why? **Award 1 mark for a plausible emotion and explanation.** **Skill: Inference.**
4 Roald goes to Africa. 4 Roald goes to boarding school. 3 Roald goes to Norway. 2 Roald moves house. 1	If the children find this challenging, encourage them to identify one key word for each statement and then scan the text to highlight these words. They should then be able to order the events. **Award 1 mark for the correct numbers in all boxes.** **Skill: Sequencing.**
5 wrote books/travelled around the world/returned home	Encourage the children to verbally explain their answers to you or their peers (e.g. *I think he went back to Norway because he liked to travel and he had fun there*). This will help you evaluate each child's understanding of prediction. If the children struggle, work as a class to find information from the text that justifies a prediction. Some children may be able to include a reason for their prediction. In this case, encourage them to provide one that is linked to the text. **Award 1 mark for a plausible prediction.** **Skill: Prediction.**

Progress check 2

Name: ______________________

1 Look at the first paragraph. Find and copy **one** word that means the same as 'well-known'.

____

1 mark

2 Look at the second paragraph. Tick **two** things that **were** around back then.

cars ☐

cinema ☐

sweet shops ☐

television ☐

1 mark

3 Look at the last sentence. How do you think Roald felt when he went to Africa? How do you know?

____

____

____

1 mark

4 Number the events to show the order in which they happened. One has been done for you.

Roald goes to Africa. ☐

Roald goes to boarding school. ☐

Roald goes to Norway. ☐

Roald moves house. 1

1 mark

5 What do you think Roald Dahl did next?

____

____

1 mark

The Life of Roald Dahl: A Marvellous Adventure, by Emma Fischel

Have you ever heard of the author Roald Dahl? Perhaps you have read one of his books or watched a film based on one of his stories, such as *Charlie and the Chocolate Factory*. In this text, we learn all about Roald Dahl's early life.

Roald Dahl is one of the most famous children's writers ever. Even children who don't like reading very much like HIS books. Roald knew exactly what children liked to read about and how to tell a story well. That's why his books have sold millions of copies all over the world. Every day letters from children and their teachers poured through his letter box. He tried to answer them all.

Both Roald's parents were Norwegian but his father ran away from Norway when he was quite young. "I shall seek my fortune abroad," he said. By the time Roald was born his father had made lots of money. It was a good thing too, as his family was rather big. Then sad times hit the family. Roald's father and one of his sisters died within months of each other. The family moved to a smaller house which Roald loved. When he was six he went to his first school – by tricycle. There weren't many cars on the road back then. There was no television either, no videos and no cinema. But there WERE sweet shops.

Roald and his family spent exciting summers in Norway. It took four days to get there by train and boat. Back at home, Roald's mother said, "Now you are nine, it's time you went away to school. English boarding schools are the best of all!" Roald didn't think so, though. At thirteen he went to another school but that was even worse. Younger boys had to be servants to older ones. Roald didn't get on with many of the teachers – and they didn't get on with him. He didn't like the rules and refused to bully the small boys. He was made captain of two sports teams but that still didn't make him popular. Not all the teachers were bad though.

At last, school was over. "And now, to university," said his mother.

"Not likely!" said Roald. "I shall become a businessman and travel the world."

"We are sending you to Egypt," said one of his bosses two years later.

"Too dusty!" said Roald. "And I'd like some jungles, please."

In the end they sent him to East Africa. Roald reached Africa at last. "So much to see," he said. "So different from home!"

George's Marvellous Medicine

by Roald Dahl

Printable text • Modelling slides   Photocopiable text and questions • pages 132 to 135

Ask anyone to name a classic children's author and one of their answers is likely to be Roald Dahl. While the text in Progress check 2, *The Life of Roald Dahl: A Marvellous Adventure*, taught the children about the author's life, while this text introduces them to his wicked and wonderful writing style through an extract from one of his most popular books, *George's Marvellous Medicine*. In this text, George is left at home with his 'grouch' of a grandma. The familiar domestic setting allows young readers to engage with Dahl's brilliant characters and sense of humour.

1 Get ready

Discuss the **Key vocabulary** identified in the **Language toolkit** and then complete the vocabulary and phonics activities as desired. Please note that the selected vocabulary is a guide. Depending on the needs of your cohort, additional vocabulary discussion may be beneficial before, during and after reading. Next, display the text (pages 132 to 133) so the children can see the title and any illustrations, and encourage the children to discuss the following questions before reading.

1. **What type of text is this? How do you know?**
   Fiction. The children should be able to explain the features of a fictional text.
2. **What facts do you already know about Roald Dahl's life?**
   Answers will vary but should relate to the text and discussion in Progress check 2 if this has been completed.
3. **Have you ever read a book by Roald Dahl? If so, which one?**
   Answers will vary depending on the children's exposure to texts by Dahl (e.g. *Matilda*, *The Minpins*, *The Magic Finger*).
4. **This story is about a boy spending some time with his grandma. Tell me about something fun that you have done with one of your relatives.**
   Answers will vary. This will be useful to contrast with Dahl's portrayal of George's grandma. Care should be taken with this question if any of your cohort have recently suffered a bereavement.

Language toolkit

Key vocabulary

childish	disobedience	greed
griping	grouching	grousing
grumbling	laziness	ridiculous
rim	saucer	sloppiness

Vocabulary discussion questions

- Can a grown-up be **childish**?
- Is **laziness** the same as **sloppiness**?
- If something is **ridiculous**, is it good or bad?

Vocabulary activities

1. The author uses lots of synonyms for 'complaining'. Ask the children how many they can find in the text.
2. Use one of the vocabulary activities on page 15 to investigate some of the key words above.

Phonics

Longer words	**disobedience, extremely, grandmothers, laziness, miserable, ridiculous, sloppiness, stupidity, untidiness**
Common exception words	**again, even, every, fast, father, kind, most, old, only, people, sugar, who**

Phonics activity

This text includes some longer words. Ask the children to work with a partner to clap and count the syllables of these words before writing down the phonemes they hear.

2 First steps

Read the text together and then encourage the children to discuss the following questions.

1 **Where do you think the story is set? Why?**
Answers will vary between George's house and Grandma's house. Ensure the children justify their opinions using the text (e.g. *It says he went into the kitchen*).

2 **What is the main event in the story?**
George making a cup of tea for his grandma.

3 **Do you like the two main characters? Why? Why not?**
Answers will vary but it is likely that the children will respond positively to George and negatively to Grandma. Ensure the children justify their opinions using the text (e.g. *I didn't like Grandma because she says mean things to George such as he's lazy*).

4 **Did you like the text? Why? Why not?**
Answers will vary. Encourage the children to explain their answers (e.g. *I liked it because I want to know what happens next*).

3 Explore

- Many of Roald Dahl's stories feature the main character, a child, being treated badly by an adult and then getting their revenge. Discuss times when the children have been treated badly by other people. How did they deal with it in a positive way, rather than trying to get their revenge? You could link this discussion to the children's knowledge of Guy Fawkes' actions from Unit 4.
- Roald Dahl made villains very obvious in his stories. Discuss what language Dahl uses to make Grandma the villain. Ask the children to imagine that they are the author. What else could they say about Grandma to make her even more villainous?
- Show the children the blurbs for some of Roald Dahl's other stories. Can they pick out the hero and the villain from each story? How are they similar or different to George and Grandma?

4 Skills focus

See pages 130 to 131

Use the information from the **Skills guide** and the relevant **Skills graphic** to introduce the skill of retrieval.

1 Model the skill using the **Unit 13 Modelling slides** and the **Modelling retrieval** guidance on page 130.

2 The children can then attempt the **Retrieval** questions on page 134.

3 Finally, the **Mix it up!** questions on page 135 offer practice in a range of comprehension skills.

Answers and marking guidance for all questions are included on pages 130 to 131.

5 Where next?

- Speaking and listening task: The children could work together in small groups to improvise a sketch of George and Grandma on another day. Discuss how the children can show both characters through their speech and mannerisms.
- Writing task: The children could create recipes together for a special tea for Grandma. They could even add their own secret ingredients to make the tea taste even better … or to get their revenge.

Reading list

Fiction

- *How to Babysit a Grandma* by Jean Reagan
- *Professor Puffendorf's Secret Potions* by Robin Tzannes
- *The Truth About Old People* by Elina Ellis

Class reads

- *The Magic Finger* by Roald Dahl

Non-fiction

- *Edible Science: Experiments You Can Eat* by Jodi Wheeler-Toppen
- *George's Marvellous Experiments* by Jim Peacock
- *The Life of Roald Dahl: A Marvellous Adventure* by Emma Fischel (Linked text: Progress check 2)

Poetry

- *How to Turn Your Teacher Purple! Sizzling Science Poems* by James Carter
- *Revolting Rhymes* by Roald Dahl

TV series

- 'George's Marvellous Medicine', *Jackanory*, BBC (2007)

Modelling retrieval

See Unit 13 Modelling slides

Use the **Skills guide** (see pages 16 to 17) and the downloadable **Skills graphic** to support your modelling.

1 How much sugar did Grandma want in her tea?

one spoon(ful)

Read the question together and model identifying the key words ('much', 'sugar', 'grandma', 'tea') and scanning for them in the text to find the relevant section. Then model using 'Fastest finger first' (see page 17) to show the answer within the text. Some children may answer vaguely (e.g. 'one'). In this case, ask them to expand on this by thinking aloud: *Is it one banana? One centimetre? What does the text actually say?*

2 Look at the paragraph beginning *Most grandmothers* . . . . Name two things Grandma was always doing.

sitting in her chair by the window and complaining

Read the question together and emphasise that we need to find two pieces of information. Model using the locator to find the relevant paragraph and reading it closely to find the answer. Model scanning for the key words in the text (e.g. 'always') and using 'Fastest finger first'. If the children respond with any of the synonyms for 'complaining' that are in the text (e.g. 'grousing', 'grouching'), check that they can explain the meaning of these words.

3 Look at the section beginning *George went into the kitchen* . . . . What did Grandma think about the tea at first? Tick one.

It needed more milk. ☐
It was too hot. ☐
It needed more sugar. ☑
It needed a saucer. ☐

Read the question together and model using the locator to find the correct section. Model scanning for the key words and using 'Fastest finger first' to show the answer within the text. The children may select 'It needed a saucer', as this comes up later on. In this case, refocus them on the key word 'first'. You could model highlighting the key words in the text and then pointing to the first one that occurs.

4 Tick to show whether each statement is true or false.

	True	False
Grandma was mean to George.	✓	
Grandma asked George how he was.		✓
George made Grandma a cup of tea.	✓	

Read the question together. If necessary, discuss the words 'true' and 'false'. You could relate this to facts about the children. Think aloud: *Your name is Daniel. True or false?* Model using the key words from the statements and 'Fastest finger first' to find the answers. Model failing to find the answer for the false statement, explaining that the statement must not be true. Finally, explicitly model ticking the correct boxes, thinking aloud to support children's understanding.

Retrieval questions mark scheme

See page 134

Answer	Guidance
1 none/no	Some children may confuse the milk with the spoon of sugar, as Grandma's comment about milk is in response to a question about sugar. In this case, prompt them to reread the second sentence and check their response. **Award 1 mark for any reference to 'none' or 'no'.**

Answer	Guidance
2 (more) sugar/(a) saucer/(a) teaspoon	Some children will need reminding to name two items. **Award 1 mark for two correct answers. Do not accept references to the tea bag or milk.**
3 when they were on their own ✓	If the children select 'all the time', remind them to use the locator and check their response. **Award 1 mark for the correct answer ticked.**
4 He was growing too fast. ✓	The children may select 'He was lazy' as Grandma used this word to describe boys who grow too fast. In this case, ask them to reread the sentence. Think aloud: *What does Grandma say about George in particular?* You could encourage them to look for the words 'you' or 'you're'. **Award 1 mark for the correct answer ticked.**
5 8/eight years old	This question is quite challenging as it does not include a locator. Some children may benefit from being given a locator but most should be able to find the information by scanning the text for a number. If necessary, you could prompt them. **Award 1 mark for any reference to eight years old. Also accept references to just the number, without the clarification of measurement.**

Mix it up! questions mark scheme

See page 135

Answer	Guidance
1 no milk ✓ one spoon of sugar ✓	If necessary, support the children by providing a locator. **Award 1 mark for the correct answers ticked.** Skill: Retrieval.
2 kind *OR* helpful	If the children answer with 'lovely', discuss the definition of this word. Think aloud: *If someone is lovely, does that definitely mean they are caring?* If the children respond with more than one word, remind them that the question asks for only one word and help them to shorten their response. **Award 1 mark for a correct answer. Do not accept answers of more than one word.** Skill: Word meaning.
3 upset/angry/annoyed	Encourage the children to verbally explain their choice of emotion to check their understanding. **Award 1 mark for any reference to a plausible emotion.** Skill: Inference.
4 George made a cup of tea. 1 George fetched a saucer. 3 George fetched a teaspoon. 4 George added more sugar to the tea. 2	If the children find this challenging, encourage them to scan the text for each event and highlight it. This will help them to order the events. **Award 1 mark for the correct numbers in all boxes.** Skill: Sequencing.
5 I think George will run away because his grandma won't stop being mean to him and he might want to get away from her.	Encourage the children to justify their explanations using the text. **Award 1 mark for a plausible prediction and 1 mark for an appropriate explanation.** Skill: Prediction.

George's Marvellous Medicine, by Roald Dahl

In this extract, George is trying, and failing, to make his mean grandma a cup of tea.

"How much sugar in your tea today, Grandma?" George asked her.

"One spoon," she said. "And no milk."

Most grandmothers are lovely, kind, helpful old ladies, but not this one. She spent all day and every day sitting in her chair by the window, and she was always complaining, grousing, grouching, grumbling, griping about something or other. Never once, even on her best days, had she smiled at George and said, "Well, how are you this morning, George?" or "Why don't you and I have a game of Snakes and Ladders?" or "How was school today?" She didn't seem to care about other people, only about herself. She was a miserable old grouch.

George went into the kitchen and made Grandma a cup of tea with a teabag. He put one spoon of sugar in it and no milk. He stirred the sugar well and carried the cup into the living-room.

Grandma sipped the tea. "It's not sweet enough," she said. "Put more sugar in it."

George took the cup back to the kitchen and added another spoonful of sugar. He stirred it again and carried it carefully in to Grandma.

"Where's the saucer?" she said. "I won't have a cup without a saucer."

George fetched her a saucer.

"And what about a teaspoon, if you please?"

"I've stirred it for you, Grandma. I stirred it well."

"I'll stir my own tea, thank you very much," she said. "Fetch me a teaspoon."

George fetched her a teaspoon.

When George's mother or father were home, Grandma never ordered George about like this. It was only when she had him on her own that she began treating him badly.

"You know what's the matter with you?" the old woman said, staring at George over the rim of the teacup with those bright wicked little eyes. "You're growing too fast. Boys who grow too fast become stupid and lazy."

"But I can't help it if I am growing fast, Grandma," George said.

"Of course you can," she snapped. "Growing's a nasty childish habit."

"But we have to grow, Grandma. If we didn't grow, we'd never be grown-ups."

"Rubbish, boy, rubbish," she said. "Look at me. Am I growing? Certainly not."

"But you did once, Grandma."

"Only very little," the old woman answered. "I gave up growing when I was extremely small, along with all the other nasty childish habits like laziness and disobedience and greed and sloppiness and untidiness and stupidity. You haven't given up any of these things, have you?"

"I'm still only a little boy, Grandma."

"You're eight years old," she snorted. "That's old enough to know better. If you don't stop growing soon, it'll be too late."

"Too late for what, Grandma?"

"It's ridiculous," she went on. "You're nearly as tall as me already."

Retrieval

Name: ______________________

1 How much milk did Grandma want in her tea?

______________________ 1 mark

2 Look at the section beginning *George went into the kitchen ...* .
Name **two** things that Grandma asked George to get for her tea.

______________________ and ______________________ 1 mark

3 Look at the section beginning *When George's mother ...* . When did Grandma treat George badly? Tick **one**.

- all the time ☐
- when they were on their own ☐
- never ☐
- when George's mum and dad were home ☐

1 mark

4 Look at the section beginning *When George's mother ...* . What did Grandma dislike about George? Tick **one**.

- He was lazy. ☐
- He did not listen. ☐
- He was rude. ☐
- He was growing too fast. ☐

1 mark

5 How old is George?

______________________ 1 mark

Mix it up!

Name: ______________________

1 Look at the first section. What did Grandma ask for in her tea? Tick **two**.

no milk ☐

one drop of milk ☐

one spoon of sugar ☐

two spoons of sugar ☐

1 mark

2 *Most grandmothers are lovely, kind, helpful old ladies, but not this one.*
Find and copy **one** word that means the same as 'caring'.

____

1 mark

3 How do you think George felt when Grandma ordered him about?

____

1 mark

4 Number the events to show the order in which they happened in the story. One has been done for you.

George made a cup of tea. ☐

George fetched a saucer. ☐

George fetched a teaspoon. ☐

George added more sugar to the tea. 2

1 mark

5 What do you predict will happen next in the story?

I think ______________________

____

because ______________________

______________________.

2 marks

Horrid Henry and the Football Fiend

by Francesca Simon

Printable text • Modelling slides Photocopiable text and questions • pages 140 to 143

The text for this unit comes from the hugely popular *Horrid Henry* series by Francesca Simon. Young readers are sure to delight in Horrid Henry's naughty antics. In this extract, Henry falls out with his brother, Perfect Peter, and then plans his revenge. The use of humour in this text makes it an ideal pairing with *The Hundred-Mile-An-Hour Dog* (Unit 15). Once the children have completed both units, you may wish to encourage them to discuss the similarities and differences between these comic texts.

1 Get ready

Discuss the **Key vocabulary** identified in the **Language toolkit** and then complete the vocabulary and phonics activities as desired. Please note that the selected vocabulary is a guide. Depending on the needs of your cohort, additional vocabulary discussion may be beneficial before, during and after reading. Next, display the text (pages 140 to 141) so the children can see the title and any illustrations, and encourage the children to discuss the following questions before reading.

1 This story is part of a series all about a boy called Horrid Henry. Have you ever read any of the books or watched any of the television series?
Answers will vary depending on whether the children know the series. If the children enjoy this text, it is a good opportunity to hook them into reading a series of books, which can be particularly useful for more reluctant readers.

2 In this book, the main character is very naughty. Can you name any other books where the main character is naughty?
Answers will vary depending on the children's exposure to texts, but all should be able to contribute an example. As a minimum, all should recall the alternative story of 'Hansel and Gretel' from Unit 12.

3 Can you think of any other books where brothers and sisters are the main characters?
Answers will vary depending on the children's exposure to texts, but all should be able to contribute an example (they should all recall the story of 'Hansel and Gretel' from Units 11 and 12).

4 This book is very funny. Have you ever read any other really funny books?
Answers will vary depending on the children's exposure to texts, but all should be able to contribute an example.

Language toolkit

Key vocabulary

bursting	lunging	none of your business
protested	slamming	snivelled
tattle-tale	turned to ice	unfair

Vocabulary discussion questions

- If you **burst** into a room, how might you be feeling?
- Why might someone leave by **slamming** the door?
- Is being a **tattle-tale** a good or a bad thing?
- If something was **unfair**, would you **protest**?

Vocabulary activities

1 Ask the children to investigate other ways to say **turned to ice** and **none of your business**.

2 Use one of the vocabulary activities on page 15 to investigate some of the key words above.

Phonics

–less suffix	unless
Contracted forms	didn't, don't, Henry's, I've, isn't, it's, wasn't, won't, you'll, you're, you've
Longer words	annoying, assembly, computer, innocently, protested
Common exception words	class, could, every, find, hold(ing), should, told, whole

Phonics activity

How many contractions can the children find?

2 First steps

Read the text together and then encourage the children to discuss the following questions.

1 Who are the characters in this text?
(Horrid) Henry, his brother (Perfect) Peter and their mum.

2 What happens at the start of the story?
Horrid Henry goes into Perfect Peter's room and asks him what he is doing/sees that he is writing something.

3 Do you think Horrid Henry and Perfect Peter like each other? Why? Why not?
Answers will vary depending on the children's opinions. They should be encouraged to justify their ideas using the text and their own experiences, if applicable.

4 Did you like the text? Why? Why not?
Answers will vary but encourage the children to explain their answers (e.g. *I liked the part where Horrid Henry is sneaking around at the end*).

3 Explore

- Discuss who the main character in this story is and how we know this. The children may mention the title and the fact that we are privy to Henry's thoughts in phrases such as 'Horrid Henry's heart turned to ice' and 'it was so unfair'. Can the children think of some ideas for what Mum and Peter might be thinking in this text?
- Horrid Henry and his brother Perfect Peter do not always get on well. Discuss the children's relationships with their siblings, cousins or friends. Do they get on well? Do they sometimes annoy one another? What kind of things do they do to annoy each other?
- The author uses strong verbs such as 'bursting', 'slamming' and 'screamed'. Discuss possible reasons why the author, Francesca Simon, has chosen these words. What effect do they have on us, the readers? What clues do they give us about Horrid Henry's character and personality?

4 Skills focus

See pages 138 to 139

Use the information from the **Skills guide** and the relevant **Skills graphic** to introduce the skill of prediction.

1 Model the skill using the **Unit 14 Modelling slides** and the **Modelling prediction** guidance on page 138.

2 The children can then attempt the **Prediction** questions on page 142.

3 Finally, the **Mix it up!** questions on page 143 offer practice in a range of comprehension skills.

Answers and marking guidance for all questions are included on pages 138 to 139.

5 Where next?

- Speaking and listening task: The dialogue in this text lends itself to being performed. The children could perform the text as a play, working in small groups. Encourage them to pay special attention to how the characters are speaking and moving. The children could then work together to role-play being two siblings or friends arguing over something.
- Writing task: As the focus of this unit is on prediction, the children could write their own ending to the story. Will Horrid Henry stop Perfect Peter writing about him? Will Perfect Peter tell the whole school Horrid Henry's secrets? Will the brothers finally start getting on?

Reading list

Fiction

- *Dirty Bertie* by David Roberts
- *Horrid Henry Robs the Bank* by Francesca Simon
- *The Hundred-Mile-An-Hour Dog* by Jeremy Strong (Linked text: Unit 15)
- *My Best Fiend* by Sheila Lavelle
- *My Naughty Little Sister Stories* by Dorothy Edwards
- *The World's Worst Children* by David Walliams

Class reads

- *You're a Bad Man, Mr Gum!* by Andy Stanton

Non-fiction

- *Bad Kids* by Tony Robinson (extracts should be shared carefully as some material is more appropriate to Key Stage 2)
- *Horrid Henry's Joke Book* by Francesca Simon

Poetry

- *Michael Rosen's Book of Very Silly Poems* by Michael Rosen

TV series

- *Horrid Henry* (Novel Entertainment Productions, 2006–)

Modelling prediction

See Unit 14 Modelling slides

Use the **Skills guide** (see pages 22 to 23) and the downloadable **Skills graphic** to support your modelling.

1 Do you think Henry will steal the diary? Tick one. Explain your answer.

Yes ☑ No ☐

Yes – because Henry wants to know what Peter is writing about him.

Read the question together and remind the children that prediction questions often do not have locators as we are usually predicting what will happen after the story ends. You could also remind them that they need to have read and understood the whole text to be able to answer a prediction question properly, and give them an opportunity to reread the text. Emphasise that they need to use the text to give specific details to support their prediction, rather than making a guess. Discuss the fact that either answer is valid provided that it is supported by a plausible prediction.

2 The story is called *Horrid Henry and the Football Fiend*. Who do you think the football fiend is?

I think it might be someone at Henry's school.

Read the question together and model looking at the title, a feature children often miss. You may need to discuss the meaning of the word 'fiend' – you could use some of the vocabulary activities on page 15 to support this. Think aloud: *We need to think about who in the story could be a fiend.* If the children only discuss Peter and Mum, encourage them to widen their ideas in response to the meaning of the word 'fiend'.

3 Imagine Peter leaves his room at the end of the text and takes his diary with him. What do you think Horrid Henry will do next?

He will make a plan to stop Peter reading the diary in assembly.

Read the question together and model finding the end of the text. This question requires the children to engage with Henry's point of view. Encourage the children to discuss how Henry feels to help them decide what he might do next. The children's answers will vary depending on the discussion and their opinions. You could ask children to verbally justify their predictions by referring to the text, using 'Fastest finger first' (see page 17) to find the part which gives them a clue.

4 Can you think of another story about naughty children? Do you think this story will end in the same way? Why?

Horrid Henry will not end like 'Hansel and Gretel' because his mum will tell him off.

Read the question together and point out that the question is asking two different things. Discuss the first part of the question and think of a number of different texts. Choose one together and then model your thought process for the second part of the question. If the children struggle to think of texts, you could use 'Hansel and Gretel' by Bethan Woollvin from Unit 12.

Prediction questions mark scheme

See page 142

Answer	Guidance
1 He'd shout for Mum.	The children should be able to draw on the text to scaffold their prediction here. Encourage them to verbally justify their ideas (e.g. *Peter would shout for Mum because he always does that*). **Award 1 mark for a plausible prediction.**
2 Go to your room, Henry. I told you not to do this. ☑	The children are encountering this question type for the first time here, therefore they may need reminding of the strategies they could use. It is essentially a normal tick-box question; however, it is asking about speech rather than actions. Encourage the children to verbally justify their response to check understanding. **Award 1 mark for the correct answer ticked.**

Answer		Guidance
3	He was writing in his diary.	Some children may respond with a prediction based on their extrinsic knowledge here (e.g. *He was playing with his toys*). If the prediction is not based on the text, discuss the prediction and justification with the children and encourage them to use the text to support their answer. **Award 1 mark for a plausible prediction.**
4	Henry is going to wait for his brother to leave his room and then snatch the diary.	Some children may attempt to connect the title – *Horrid Henry and the Football Fiend* – to their prediction. In this case, their predictions may appear very different to others'; however, they should be accepted if plausible. **Award 1 mark for a plausible prediction.**
5	It will say that Henry is horrible to him.	The predictions provided are likely to be varied. The important thing is that they are linked to the text. If a child provides an unusual prediction, check their understanding of the text by asking them to verbally justify their prediction. **Award 1 mark for a plausible prediction.**

Mix it up! questions mark scheme

See page 143

Answer		Guidance
1	Miss Lovely	Some children may respond with a reference to 'his teacher'. As this is a retrieval question, we would not normally accept using inference. Remind the children that we need to retrieve directly from the text. **Award 1 mark for the correct answer.** Skill: Retrieval.
2	worried (circled)	Some children may choose 'cold' due to the reference to Henry's heart turning to ice. If so, discuss the meaning of the phrase 'turned to ice' again – it is not literal. If the children find this question challenging, encourage them to put themselves in Henry's shoes – how would they feel if their sibling or friend was going to tell the whole school lies about them? **Award 1 mark for the correct answer circled.** Skill: Inference.
3	He opened the diary.	Some children may respond by saying he didn't read a single word, from the following sentence. In this case, prompt them to reread the question to find something Henry **did** do. In addition, some may say he 'grabbed' the diary; however, that is from the third paragraph. In this case, remind them to check that they have used the locator. **Award 1 mark for any reference to opening the diary.** Skill: Sequencing.
4	snatched (underlined)	Some children may need to be reminded of synonym substitution and how it can help to answer questions such as this. **Award 1 mark for the correct answer underlined.** Skill: Word meaning.
5	Sneaking around ✓	Encourage the children to verbally justify their prediction using the text to check their understanding. This is especially important when they have seemingly chosen the incorrect option as their justification will allow you to see their thought process and level of understanding. **Award 1 mark for the correct answer ticked.** Skill: Prediction.

Horrid Henry and the Football Fiend, by Francesca Simon

In this extract, Horrid Henry and his brother Perfect Peter have a fight about Peter's diary.

"What are you doing?" demanded Horrid Henry, bursting into Peter's bedroom.

"Nothing," said Perfect Peter quickly, slamming his notebook shut.

"Yes, you are," said Henry.

"Get out of my room," said Peter. "You're not allowed to come in unless I say so."

Horrid Henry leaned over Peter's shoulder.

"What are you writing?"

"None of your business," said Peter. He covered the closed notebook tightly with his arm.

"It is too my business if you're writing about me."

"It's my diary. I can write what I want to," said Peter. "Miss Lovely said we should keep a diary for a week and write in it every day."

"Bo-ring," said Henry, yawning.

"No, it isn't," said Peter. "Anyway, you'll find out next week what I'm writing: I've been chosen to read my diary out loud for our class assembly."

Horrid Henry's heart turned to ice. Peter read his diary out loud? So the whole school could hear Peter's lies about him? No way!

"Gimme that!" screamed Horrid Henry, lunging for the diary.

"No!" screamed Peter, holding on tight. "MUUUM! Help! Henry's in my room! And he didn't knock! And he won't leave!"

"Shut up, tattle-tale," hissed Henry, forcing Peter's fingers off the diary.

"MUUUUMMMMMMM!" shrieked Peter.

Mum stomped up the stairs. Henry opened the diary. But before he could read a single word Mum burst in.

"He snatched my diary! And he told me to shut up!" wailed Peter.

"Henry! Stop annoying your brother," said Mum.

"I wasn't," said Henry.

"Yes he was," snivelled Peter.

"And now you've made him cry," said Mum. "Say sorry."

"I was just asking about his homework," protested Henry innocently.

"He was trying to read my diary," said Peter.

"Henry!" said Mum. "Don't be horrid. A diary is private. Now leave your brother alone."

It was so unfair. Why did Mum always believe Peter?

Humph. Horrid Henry stalked out of Peter's bedroom. Well, no way was Henry waiting until class assembly to find out what Peter had written.

Sneak. Sneak. Sneak.

Horrid Henry checked to the right. Horrid Henry checked to the left. Mum was downstairs working on the computer.

Prediction

Name: ______________________

1 Look at the whole text. What do you think Peter would do if he caught Henry sneaking around in his room?

____

______________________ 1 mark

2 Which of these do you think Mum might say if she found Henry in Peter's room again? Tick **one**.

Go to your room, Henry. I told you not to do this. ☐

Well done, Henry. ☐

Peter, why is Henry here? ☐

She would say nothing. ☐

1 mark

3 What do you think Peter was doing in his room at the end of the story?

____

______________________ 1 mark

4 What do you think Henry is most likely to do next?

____

______________________ 1 mark

5 Imagine Henry gets to read Peter's diary. What do you think it might say?

____

______________________ 1 mark

Mix it up!

Name: ______________________

1 Look at the section beginning *Horrid Henry leaned over ...* . Who told Peter to write a diary?

____ 1 mark

2 *Horrid Henry's heart turned to ice. Peter read his diary out loud? So the whole school could hear Peter's lies about him? No way!*

How did Henry feel at this point in the story? Circle **one**.

cold	happy	worried	bored

1 mark

3 Look at the section beginning *Mum stomped ...* . What did Horrid Henry do before Mum burst in?

____ 1 mark

4 Look at the sentences below. Underline **one** word that means the same as 'grabbed'.

> Mum stomped up the stairs. Henry opened the diary. But before he could read a single word Mum burst in. "He snatched my diary! And he told me to shut up!" wailed Peter.

1 mark

5 What do you think the next chapter is most likely to be called? Tick **one**.

Helping Mum ☐

Writing a diary ☐

Playing with Peter ☐

Sneaking around ☐

1 mark

The Hundred-Mile-An-Hour Dog

by Jeremy Strong

Printable text • Modelling slides   Photocopiable text and questions • pages 148 to 151

This text is by a popular author, Jeremy Strong, who is known for his comedic style of writing. In the text, we are introduced to Streaker, 'the hundred-mile-an-hour dog', who nobody wants to take for a walk, and the young boy, Trevor, who owns her. This text is linked to the Unit 14 text, *Horrid Henry*, because of its use of humour. Once both units have been completed, you may wish to discuss the links between the two texts and encourage the children to compare and contrast the characters of Trevor and Henry.

1 Get ready

Discuss the **Key vocabulary** identified in the **Language toolkit** and then complete the vocabulary and phonics activities as desired. Please note that the selected vocabulary is a guide. Depending on the needs of your cohort, additional vocabulary discussion may be beneficial before, during and after reading. Next, display the text (pages 148 to 149) so the children can see the title and any illustrations, and encourage the children to discuss the following questions before reading.

1. The author of this story is known for writing funny books that make readers laugh. Can you name any other funny books or authors?
   The children should be able to contribute examples, although this will depend on their exposure to different texts. However, all the children should be able to make a link to the Unit 14 text, *Horrid Henry*.
2. This book is funny. What do you think makes a book funny?
   Answers will vary but the children are likely to refer to the author's use of language, silly events and jokes. Some of the children may need support to articulate their response here.
3. The story is about a boy and his dog. Do you have any pets? If so, what are they? If not, do you know anyone who does?
   Answers will vary but most children should be able to discuss their own pet or that of a family member or friend. You may wish to make reference to any school pets where relevant.
4. In this story, Trevor is asked to do a job for his mum during the holidays. Do you ever have to do jobs for your parents? If so, what jobs? When are you asked to do them?
   Answers will vary but all children should be able to contribute to the discussion. If any of the children struggle to contribute, you could open this out to jobs they are asked to do around the classroom.

Language toolkit

Key vocabulary

accelerate	bribery	glare
hurtling	innocent	point-blank
twigged	vanished	whirlwind

Vocabulary discussion questions

- When would you **glare** at someone?
- Have you ever been accused of something even though you were **innocent**?
- Has anyone ever used **bribery** to get you to do something?

Vocabulary activities

1. **Hurtling** describes a fast movement. How many similar words can the children think of?
2. In addition to the words above, you may wish to use images to discuss the meaning of concrete nouns such as 'torpedo' and 'meteorite' if the children are not already familiar with the terms.

Phonics

Longer words	accelerate, beginning, bribery, controlling, craziest, decision, horizon, innocent, meteorite, nightmares, powerful, similar, surprising
Common exception words	after, both, could, even, every, eye, hour, kind, money, only, should, whole, would

Phonics activity

This story includes lots of longer words, such as **innocent**. How many can the children find?

2 First steps

Read the text together and then encourage the children to discuss the following questions.

1 **Who are the characters in this text? Of these, who are the most important?**
Streaker, Trevor, Mum and Dad. Streaker, Trevor and Mum are the most important as they all play a role in this extract; Dad is only mentioned by Trevor. The children may also focus on their idea of the central character (e.g. Streaker because the book is named after her).

2 **Where and when is the story set?**
At Trevor's house, during the Easter holidays. You may also want to discuss that the text is set approximately in the present day and discuss the clues, such as the mention of TV, that lead us to this conclusion.

3 **What name is Streaker also known by? Why?**
The Hundred-Mile-an-Hour Dog, because she is incredibly fast.

4 **Did you like the text? Why? Why not?**
Answers will vary but encourage the children to explain their answers (e.g. *I liked it because Streaker seems like she might cause chaos*).

3 Explore

- Ask the children whether they have ever been asked to do something they did not want to do, like Trevor. How did they handle this? Did they do as they were asked? Why, or why not? You could focus on shared contexts (e.g. classroom playground) here.
- In humorous stories like this one, there is often lots of physical humour, as when Streaker jumps on to Trevor's lap and they both fall over. Discuss similar experiences the children have had. Why were they funny?
- The author uses descriptive language to describe Streaker and her behaviour, such as 'the hundred-mile-an-hour dog' and 'out-accelerate a torpedo'. Discuss how we could describe other animals using similar language (e.g. for an elephant: lumbering giant; plodding like a brachiosaurus; a tree-like trunk).

4 Skills focus

See pages 146 to 147

Use the information from the **Skills guide** and the relevant **Skills graphic** to introduce the skill of word meaning.

1 Model the skill using the **Unit 15 Modelling slides** and the **Modelling Word meaning** guidance on page 146.

2 The children can then attempt the **Word meaning** questions on page 150.

3 Finally, the **Mix it up!** questions on page 151 offer practice in a range of comprehension skills.

Answers and marking guidance for all questions are included on pages 146 to 147.

5 Where next?

- Speaking and listening task: The children could role-play the conversation between Trevor and his mum, thinking about how they would react in his situation. Would they take the money and walk Streaker every day, even though they did not want to, or would they refuse? They could extend this drama activity to show their predictions about what might happen next. Would Streaker cause chaos? Or would walking her turn out to be a great activity for Trevor?
- Writing task: The children could work together in groups to research how to look after a range of pets. You could focus on unusual pets (e.g. lizards, ferrets, snakes) or perhaps the school pet, if you are lucky enough to have one. Produce information posters to help people look after their pets properly and keep them safe and happy.

Reading list

Fiction

- *Barry Loser and the Trouble with Pets* by Jim Smith
- *Dog Diaries* by Steven Butler and James Patterson
- *Horrid Henry and the Football Fiend* by Francesca Simon (Linked text: Unit 14)
- *Some Pets* by Angela DiTerlizzi
- *Wolf Camp* by Andrea Zuill

Class reads

- *My Dad's Got an Alligator!* by Jeremy Strong

Non-fiction

- *Amazing Dogs* by Laura Buller
- *The Funny Life of Pets* by James Campbell
- *National Geographic Kids: 125 True Stories of Amazing Animals* by National Geographic

Poetry

- *Pet Poems* by Jennifer Curry

Films

- *The Secret Life of Pets* (Universal Pictures, 2016)

Modelling word meaning

See Unit 15 Modelling slides

Use the **Skills guide** (see pages 14 to 15) and the downloadable **Skills graphic** to support your modelling.

1 ***You can see from her thin body and powerful legs that she's got a lot of greyhound blood in her, along with quite a bit of Ferrari and a large chunk of whirlwind.* Find and copy one word which means the same as 'big'.**

large

Read the question together and model identifying the key words before scanning the sentence together. Point out that the question asks us to find just one word. Some children might answer 'powerful' or 'a lot of'. In this case, discuss the meaning of 'powerful'. Think aloud: *Can an ant be powerful even though it is not big?* If children answer 'a lot of', remind them that the question asks for one word only.

2 ***Mum gave me a chilly glare. Glare* means that Mum was feeling … Tick one.**

happy ☐ sad ☐ annoyed ☑ proud ☐

Read the question together and model identifying the key words and using the locator to scan for the correct sentence. Discuss the synonyms for 'chilly' to help the children find the correct answer. If the children struggle, run a short drama activity to explore what glaring looks like and when we might glare at someone instead of simply looking at them.

3 ***"Trevor …" said Mum one morning at the beginning of the holiday, and she gave me one of her really big, innocent smiles.* Underline one word which means the same as 'start'.**

beginning

Read the question together and model identifying the key words. Encourage the children to see if they can think of a word that means the same as 'start'. Ensure that you explicitly model looking for the synonym in the sentence and underlining it when you have found it.

4 **Look at the last paragraph. How did Mum pedal? Tick one.**

quickly ☐ slowly ☐ loudly ☐ silently ☑

Read the question together and model using the locator to find the relevant paragraph. Then model identifying the key words (e.g. 'Mum', 'pedal') and scanning the text for these. This question requires children to link 'quietly' to 'silently'. You could generate some synonyms together before attempting the question.

Word meaning questions mark scheme

See page 150

Answer	Guidance
1 yell	Some children may answer using more than one word. In this case, remind them that the question asks for one word only. If the children struggle, discuss some synonyms for 'shout' together. **Award 1 mark for the correct answer.**
2 once a day ☑	This question requires the children to understand the link between 'every day' and 'once a day'. If they struggle, focus them on the relevant sentence. This will reduce the cognitive load and still allow them to show their understanding of vocabulary. **Award 1 mark for the correct answer ticked.**
3 important ☑	This is a tricky question with a strong distractor ('large'), which features in **Modelling question 1**. If necessary, encourage the children to substitute each possible answer into the target sentence to see which makes most sense. Remind them that many words have multiple meanings. **Award 1 mark for the correct answer ticked.**

Answer		Guidance
4	It means humans are in charge or are the king of the animals.	You may wish to provide tick-box options for any children who struggle to articulate their understanding here. If they use the alternative meaning of 'rule' (i.e. something that you have to stick by), explain the need to use the context to support our understanding, and that 'rule' here is a verb and not a noun. **Award 1 mark for any reference to humans being in charge or being the king of the animals.**
5	slipped	If the children give answers of more than one word (e.g. 'slipped off'), do not accept this. You could use these as a teaching point for the class. Refocus the children on the question wording and point out that even though 'slipped off' contains the correct word, it does not meet the question's expectations. **Award 1 mark for the correct answer underlined.**

Mix it up! questions mark scheme

See page 151

Answer		Guidance
1	because Trevor said 'she' and 'her' when talking about Streaker	This is a challenging inference question because it relies on coherence inferences (see page 20 of the **Skills guide**) which normally happen automatically. If necessary, support the children by highlighting the pronouns in the text and asking the children what they tell us. **Award 1 mark for any reference to the fact that Trevor referred to her as 'she' and 'her' (female pronouns).** Skill: Inference.
2	at the start of the holiday ☑	Some children may scan for the word 'start' when in fact its synonym 'beginning' is used. If they struggle, you may wish to help them by changing the wording of the answer from 'start' to 'beginning' to follow the wording used in the text. **Award 1 mark for the correct answer ticked.** Skill: Retrieval.
3	She was on her exercise bike./She was pedalling./She was on her bike.	Support the children by giving them a locator (fourth paragraph) if needed. If the children find this question challenging, remind them of the advice from the **Skills graphic** and encourage them to identify and locate the key words (e.g. 'Mum', 'talked', 'Trevor'). **Award 1 mark for any reference to being on the exercise bike, including responses involving pedalling, exercising or vague responses to being on her bike.** Skill: Sequencing.
4	pleased	Some children may answer 'pleased with herself'. In this case, refocus them on the question's expectations and the rules of 'find and copy' questions. Encourage them to remove extraneous detail until they are left with only one word. **Award 1 mark for the correct answer.** Skill: Word meaning.
5	Yes – because he really wants the money. *OR* No – because he doesn't like doing it.	If the children struggle to produce a written justification, encourage them to verbally justify their prediction or use a graphic organiser (see page 23) to structure their response. **Award 1 mark for a plausible prediction.** Skill: Prediction.

The Hundred-Mile-An-Hour Dog, by Jeremy Strong

This text is from a funny book by Jeremy Strong, about a boy called Trevor and his dog Streaker. Streaker is such a fast dog that no one wants to take her for a walk, but Trevor's mum has a plan ...

Streaker is a mixed-up kind of dog. You can see from her thin body and powerful legs that she's got a lot of greyhound blood in her, along with quite a bit of Ferrari and a large chunk of whirlwind. Nobody in our family likes walking her and this is hardly surprising. Streaker can out-accelerate a torpedo. She can do 0 to 100mph in the blink of an eye. She's usually vanished over the far horizon long before you have time to yell – "Streaker!"

Dad refuses to walk her, point-blank. "I've got backache," is his usual excuse, though how this stops him from walking I really haven't a clue. I tried something similar once myself. "I've got front-ache," I said. Mum gave me a chilly glare and handed me the dog-lead. She'll do anything to get out of walking Streaker too, and that is how the whole thing started. I ended up having the craziest Easter holiday you can imagine.

"Trevor ..." said Mum one morning at the beginning of the holiday, and she gave me one of her really big, innocent smiles. "Trevor ..." (I should have guessed she was up to something); "Trevor – I'll give you thirty pounds if you walk Streaker every day this holiday." Thirty pounds! As you can imagine, my eyes boggled a bit. I just about had to shove them back in their sockets. I was so astonished I never twigged that what my mother was suggesting was MAJOR BRIBERY.

"It's the Easter holiday," she continued, climbing on to her exercise-bike and pulling a pink sweat band round her forehead. "You've nothing better to do." "Thirty pounds?" I repeated. "Walk her every day for two weeks?" Mum nodded and began to pedal. I sat down to have a think. Thirty pounds was a lot of money. I could do loads of things with that. On the other hand – and this was the big crunch – I would have to walk Streaker. Now, if someone came up to you in the street and said, "Hey! What's the worst torture you can think of?", you might suggest boiling in oil, or having to watch golf on TV with your dad, or even the nine times table – which is one of my own personal nightmares. But without doubt I would have to say – walking Streaker. This was going to be a big decision for me.

I reckoned there had to be some way of controlling Streaker. After all, she was only a dog. Humans are cleverer than animals. Humans have bigger brains. Humans rule the animal kingdom. I seem to remember that just as I was thinking this, Streaker came hurtling in from the kitchen and landed on my lap like a mini-meteorite. We both crashed to the floor, where she sat on my chest looking very pleased with herself. Mum carried on quietly pedalling all this time. She must have known I'd give in. "I'll do it," I said. Mum gave a strange squeak and one of her feet slipped off a pedal. For some reason she looked even more pleased with herself than Streaker did.

Word meaning

Name: ____________________

1 *She's usually vanished over the far horizon long before you have time to yell – "Streaker!"*
Find and copy **one** word that means the same as 'shout'.

____________________ 1 mark

2 Look at the third paragraph. How often did Trevor have to walk Streaker? Tick **one**.

once ☐

once a day ☐

every week ☐

once a year ☐

1 mark

3 *This was going to be a big decision for me.*
Which of these words is closest to the meaning of *big* here? Tick **one**.

important ☐

large ☐

easy ☐

boring ☐

1 mark

4 *Humans rule the animal kingdom.*
What does the word *rule* mean here?

____________________ 1 mark

5 Look at the sentence below. Underline **one** word that tells you Mum's foot fell off a pedal.

Mum gave a strange squeak and one of her feet slipped off a pedal.

1 mark

Mix it up!

Name: ____________________

1 Streaker is a female dog. How do you know?

____

______________________________ 1 mark

2 Look at the third paragraph. When did Mum talk to Trevor? Tick **one**.

at the weekend ☐

at the end of the holiday ☐

at the start of the holiday ☐

on Tuesday ☐

1 mark

3 What was Mum doing at the same time as talking to Trevor?

______________________________ 1 mark

4 *For some reason she looked even more pleased with herself than Streaker did.*
Find and copy **one** word that means the same as 'happy'.

______________________________ 1 mark

5 Do you think Trevor will walk Streaker every day? Tick **one**.

Yes ☐ No ☐

Why?

____

______________________________ 1 mark

The Darkest Dark

by Chris Hadfield

Printable text • Modelling slides   Photocopiable text and questions • pages 156 to 159

Children are natural explorers. Many of them, no doubt, dream of travelling into space or having an adventure on the moon. The author of this text, Chris Hadfield, is a real-life astronaut. In this text, he tells a fictional story based on his own childhood, about a little boy who is fascinated by space but terrified of the dark. In our next text, Unit 17, we will learn about the canine adventurers who went into space before humans. When both units are completed, you may wish to make links between the two texts.

1 Get ready

Discuss the **Key vocabulary** identified in the **Language toolkit** and then complete the vocabulary and phonics activities as desired. Please note that the selected vocabulary is a guide. Depending on the needs of your cohort, additional vocabulary discussion may be beneficial before, during and after reading. Next, display the text (pages 156 to 157) so the children can see the title and any illustrations, and encourage the children to discuss the following questions before reading.

1 What type of text is this? How do you know?
The children should easily be able to identify that this is a fictional text. You may wish to explain that, although it is a story, it is based on true events – Chris Hadfield is retelling what happened to him during his childhood.

2 This story is about the first moon landing in 1969. Have you read any other books that are about the moon, or that are set in space?
Answers will vary depending on the children's exposure to different texts, but all should be able to contribute to the discussion.

3 The story is about a young boy and his dreams for the future. Have you read any other books that talk about people's hopes and dreams?
Answers will vary depending on the children's exposure to different texts, but all should be able to contribute to the discussion.

4 In the story, Chris is very excited about a special day that is coming up. When have you been really excited about something that is coming in the future?
Answers will vary but all the children should be able to contribute their own examples (e.g. birthdays, family celebrations).

Language toolkit

Key vocabulary

alien	astronauts	depended
experiment	gathered	gravity
huddled	mystery	universe

Vocabulary discussion questions

- Have you and your classmates ever **gathered** around anything?
- What is an **alien**? When might we say that a place, a thing or a situation is **alien** to us?
- Are we in the **universe** right now?

Vocabulary activities

1 Ask the children to role-play how **astronauts** move with no **gravity** holding them down.

2 Use one of the vocabulary activities on page 15 to investigate some of the key words above.

Phonics

–ly suffix	actually, finally, really
–ful suffix	wonderful
–ness suffix	darkness
Longer words	astronauts, expected, experiment, gravity, mystery, realised, tomorrow, universe, velvety, wonderful
Common exception words	because, could, door, even, every, kind, last, only, people, pretty, who, whole, would

Phonics activity

Can the children find any past tense verbs that **do not** end in '–ed' (e.g. 'ran')?

2 First steps

Read the text together and then encourage the children to discuss the following questions.

1 **Why was tomorrow 'a very special day'?**
People were going to land on the moon for the first time and it was going to be on the television.

2 **Where did Chris go to watch the moon landing? Why was this?**
To his neighbour's house because they had the only TV on the island.

3 **What did Chris decide he wanted to do when he was older?**
He wanted to explore every corner of the night sky and become an astronaut.

4 **Did you like the text? Why? Why not?**
Answers will vary but encourage the children to explain their answers (e.g. *I liked it because Chris followed his dreams*).

3 Explore

- In the story, Chris talks about his hopes and dreams. One day, he wants to be an astronaut and visit the blackness of outer space. Discuss what the children's hopes and dreams are for the future. You could talk about a hope for this week, this year and when they are grown up.
- We know that earlier in the story Chris was really afraid of the dark. Discuss how that changes in this text, and why. Can the children pick out any of the words that show the change? Can they relate this to their own experience – did they once feel afraid of something that doesn't bother them so much now? What changed?
- The author repeats words and phrases such as 'a special day' and 'a very special day'; 'astronauts' and 'real, live astronauts'; and 'dark', 'darkest dark' and 'very, very dark'. Discuss why you think the author does this. What effect does this have on the reader?

4 Skills focus

See pages 154 to 155

Use the information from the **Skills guide** and the relevant **Skills graphic** to introduce the skill of word meaning.

1 Model the skill using the **Unit 16 Modelling slides** and the **Modelling Word meaning** guidance on page 154.

2 The children can then attempt the **Word meaning** questions on page 158.

3 Finally, the **Mix it up!** questions on page 159 offer practice in a range of comprehension skills.

Answers and marking guidance for all questions are included on pages 154 to 155.

5 Where next?

- Speaking and listening task: Continue your discussion from the **Explore** section about the children's hopes and dreams. Discuss the excitement and amazement that Chris and the people around him feel when they watch the astronauts land on the moon. Emphasise that no one was sure that humans could achieve this at that time, and that many people worked for years to make this dream a reality. You could even link this to Martin Luther King's famous 'I Have a Dream' speech and discuss as a class your dreams for the world as a whole. The children could create a class dream box where they collect objects that symbolise their hopes and dreams for themselves and the world.
- Writing task: The author of this text, Chris Hadfield, was a real-life astronaut, though he is now retired. The children could work together to find out more about Commander Hadfield. They could even create a poster or write a non-fiction book about him and his trips into space.

Reading list

Fiction

- *Man on the Moon* by Simon Bartram

Class reads

- *One Giant Leap: The Story of Neil Armstrong* by Don Brown

Non-fiction

- *Dogs in Space* by Vix Southgate (Linked text: Unit 17)
- *The International Space Station* by Clive Gifford
- *A Journey Through Space* by Steve Parker

Poetry

- *Footprints on the Moon* by Mark Carthew
- 'Goodnight Spaceman' by Michelle Robinson

Films

- *Fly Me to the Moon* (nWave Pictures, 2008)

Modelling word meaning

See Unit 16 Modelling slides

Use the **Skills guide** (see pages 14 to 15) and the downloadable **Skills graphic** to support your modelling.

1 ***"One more peep, young man, and I'm afraid we'll all be too tired to go next door tomorrow."* What does the word *peep* mean in this sentence?**

noise/sound

Read the question together. Model using the locator and scanning for the key word 'peep'. Discuss the idea of a parent trying to get a small child to go to sleep. Think aloud: *What would they want the child to do and not do?* Discuss the fact that Chris is in bed and his parents want him to go to sleep but he is excited. Some children may relate the word 'peep' to 'looking'. If so, remind them that we need to check that the word has that meaning in this sentence. Also, remind them to use synonym substitution to help them if they do not know the meaning – what other words would 'work' instead of 'peep'?

2 ***But finally, when the Moon was shining over the lake and the summer wind was ruffling the leaves of the trees, Chris ran next door.* Which answer is closest in meaning to *finally*? Tick <u>one</u>.**

soon ☐
after a little while ☐
after a long while ☑
straight away ☐

Read the question together. Model using the locator and scanning for the key word 'finally' before reading around the word. Discuss what 'finally' means. Think aloud: *Can we remove any options which we know are incorrect?* You may need to spend some time exploring the difference between 'a little while' and 'a long while' – a timeline diagram may be helpful here.

3 ***That night, Chris did a little experiment. He turned off all the lights in his room, even the night-light.* Find and copy <u>one</u> word that means the same as *test*.**

experiment

Read the question together. Model using the locator to find the correct section in the text. Remind the children of the rules of 'find and copy' questions. Think aloud while you do this and while you model finding the answer. For example, you may wish to write the answer 'little experiment' and then verbally correct yourself after rereading the question.

4 ***He'd seen that the darkness of the universe was so much bigger and deeper than the darkness in his room, but he was not afraid.* Underline <u>one</u> word which means the same as *greater*.**

bigger

Read the question together. Model using the locator to find the correct section and identify the key words within the question. The children are unlikely to have encountered this question structure many times, so you will need to spend time exploring the instructions and modelling the written answer. Some children may think that 'deeper' is correct. If so, you should discuss the meaning of 'deeper' (e.g. in relation to the sea or a deeper colour such as dark blue, which can be called deep blue or a deeper blue).

Word meaning questions mark scheme

See page 158

Answer	Guidance
1 not moving/not making a noise/ staying asleep and not getting up	The children encountered the word 'peep' in the **Modelling questions**; however, this question requires them to think about there not being a 'peep': 'without a peep'. If they find this challenging, remind them of your previous discussion about the word 'peep'. **Award 1 mark for any reference to Chris staying asleep or not making a noise.**

Answer		Guidance
2	ruffling	As this word is uncommon and likely to be unfamiliar, you could choose to award the mark for longer responses such as 'ruffling the leaves' and 'the summer wind was ruffling the leaves'. However, care should be taken to explain that the question asks for only one word. **Award 1 mark for the correct answer.**
3	amazed	As this question structure is relatively new, you may need to remind the children of the steps needed to answer. **Award 1 mark for the correct answer. Also accept 'were amazed' but do not accept 'they'd never expected' or similar as this is a group of words.**
4	strange/weird/different	The children should have already encountered this word during your discussion of **Key vocabulary** during the **Get ready** section of this unit. If they still only see 'alien' as being a noun, spend some additional time exploring the other meaning of 'alien' as 'strange' or 'different'. **Award 1 mark for any reference to looking strange.**
5	go to ☑	Some children may answer 'see'. If so, ask them whether it is the closest in meaning to 'explore'. Continue by asking them to think about explorers: do they merely look at things or do they go to them? **Award 1 mark for the correct answer ticked.**

Mix it up! questions mark scheme

See page 159

Answer		Guidance
1	excited	Some children may provide a vague response such as 'happy'. In this case, work with them to think about different emotions and discuss whether Chris was actually only happy or if it was something more. **Award 1 mark for any reference to a plausible emotion.** **Skill: Inference.**
2	favourite	**Award 1 mark for the correct answer. Do not accept any additional words as part of a correct answer such as 'favourite dream'.** **Skill: Word meaning.**
3	Chris did an experiment. [4] Chris went to sleep. [1] Chris went next door. [2] Chris saw astronauts on the TV. [3]	Some children may choose 'Chris went to sleep' as the final option. In this case, ask them to reread the second paragraph. Think aloud: *Does it say anything about Chris going to sleep?* **Award 1 mark for the correct numbers in all boxes.** **Skill: Sequencing.**
4	astronauts jumping ☑	Some children may tick 'astronauts wearing yellow suits' as the reference to suits comes before them jumping. If so, remind them to read carefully around the key words they find when scanning the text. **Award 1 mark for the correct answer ticked.** **Skill: Retrieval.**
5	Chris went to sleep and dreamed of going to space.	Some children may predict Chris will be an astronaut. In this case, remind them how old Chris was in the story. Think aloud: *Could he be an astronaut straight away?* Encourage the children to verbally justify their prediction using the text to check their understanding. **Award 1 mark for a plausible prediction.** **Skill: Prediction.**

The Darkest Dark, by Chris Hadfield

The author of this text, Chris Hadfield, is a famous astronaut. This is an extract from a story about when Chris was a little boy dreaming of going to outer space. The only problem was that he was afraid of the dark!

"One more peep, young man, and I'm afraid we'll all be too tired to go next door tomorrow." But tomorrow would be a special day. A very special day. Chris *had* to go next door. His life pretty much depended on it. So Chris stayed in his own bed. Without a peep. It took a long time to fall asleep, but when he did, he had his favourite dream ... He flew his spaceship all the way to the Moon.

The next day seemed to last forever. But finally, when the Moon was shining over the lake and the summer wind was ruffling the leaves of the trees, Chris ran next door. The house was already full of people, all gathered around the TV – the only TV on the whole island. Chris found a spot where he could see through the crowd. And what he saw was ... astronauts. Real, live astronauts. On the actual, far-away Moon. They were wearing puffy white suits and jumping for joy – jumping so high, because there was so much less gravity there. The grown-ups huddled around the TV were amazed. Their whole lives long, they'd never expected to see this sight. Even Chris (who had been to the Moon just the night before) was amazed. He'd never really noticed how *dark* it was there. Outer space was the darkest dark ever.

That night, Chris did a little experiment. He turned off all the lights in his room, even the night-light. It was still dark. Very, *very* dark.

There were still shadows that looked a little, well, alien. Nothing had changed. But Chris had changed.

He'd seen that the darkness of the universe was so much bigger and deeper than the darkness in his room, but he was not afraid. He wanted to explore every corner of the night sky. For the first time, Chris could see the power and the mystery and velvety black beauty of the dark. And he realised you're never really alone there. Your dreams are always with you, just waiting. Big dreams, about the kind of person you want to be. Wonderful dreams about the life you will live. Dreams that actually can come true.

Word meaning

Name: ____________________

1 *So Chris stayed in his own bed. Without a peep.*
What does the group of words *without a peep* mean here?

____ 1 mark

2 *But finally, when the Moon was shining over the lake and the summer wind was ruffling the leaves of the trees ... .*
Find and copy **one** word that means the same as 'moving'.

____________________ 1 mark

3 Look at the sentences below. Underline **one** word that tells you the grown-ups were shocked.

The grown-ups huddled around the TV were amazed. Their whole lives long, they'd never expected to see this sight.

1 mark

4 *There were still shadows that looked a little, well, alien.*
What does the word *alien* mean in this sentence?

____ 1 mark

5 *He wanted to explore every corner of the night sky.*
Which answer is closest in meaning to *explore*? Tick **one**.

see ☐

draw ☐

think about ☐

go to ☐

1 mark

Mix it up!

Name: ______________________________

1 Look at the first paragraph. How did Chris feel about the next day?

____ 1 mark

2 *It took a long time to fall asleep, but when he did, he had his favourite dream ... He flew his spaceship all the way to the Moon.*
Find and copy **one** word that means the same as 'best-loved'.

______________________ 1 mark

3 Look at the first, second and third paragraphs. Number the events to show the order in which they happened in this part of the story. One has been done for you.

Chris did an experiment.	4
Chris went to sleep.	
Chris went next door.	
Chris saw astronauts on the TV.	

1 mark

4 Look at the second paragraph. What did Chris see on the TV?
Tick **one**.

astronauts waving	
astronauts wearing jumpers	
astronauts jumping	
astronauts wearing yellow suits	

1 mark

5 At the end of the story Chris was back in his bedroom. What do you think happened to Chris next?

____

____ 1 mark

Dogs in Space

by Vix Southgate

Printable text • Modelling slides Photocopiable text and questions • pages 164 to 167

When children think of space, they are likely to picture astronauts, planets, spaceships and stars. How about dogs?! This wonderful text tells the true story of Belka and Strelka, two Russian dogs who ventured into space. It is a text that is sure to interest young readers, who will be eager to hear about the space dogs' adventures. We have previously encountered space through the lens of Chris Hadfield's memories in the *The Darkest Dark* (Unit 16). You may wish to make links between these two texts during your discussion.

1 Get ready

Discuss the **Key vocabulary** identified in the **Language toolkit** and then complete the vocabulary and phonics activities as desired. Please note that the selected vocabulary is a guide. Depending on the needs of your cohort, additional vocabulary discussion may be beneficial before, during and after reading. Next, display the text (pages 164 to 165) so the children can see the title and any illustrations, and encourage the children to discuss the following questions before reading.

1 **What type of text is this? How do you know?**
This may provoke discussion as it is a non-fiction subject written as a narrative. Most of the children will probably assume it is fictional unless they already know about this episode in history.

2 **This is a true story. What does that mean? Can you think of any other examples?**
The children should be able to explain the concept of a true story; however, making links to other examples will depend on individual experience. Most children should be able to recall that *The Darkest Dark* (Unit 16) is a based on a true story if the units have been covered in order. Some of the children may also mention *The Great Fire of London* (Unit 3).

3 **Would you like to go into space? Why? Why not?**
Answers will vary but all the children should be able to contribute their own opinions and at least a simple justification.

4 **Which other books have you read that are set in space?**
Answers will vary depending on the children's exposure to texts but all should be able to make reference to the Unit 16 text, *The Darkest Dark*.

Language toolkit

Key vocabulary

cosmonauts	joy	launch
mission	monitors	orbit
platform	relief	shuddered

Vocabulary discussion questions

- What kind of person might go on a **mission**?
- Can you **launch** anything other than a rocket?
- When have you felt **relief**?

Vocabulary activities

1 Challenge the children to use dictionaries to find words with the prefixes 'astro–' and 'cosmo–' to help them understand the meaning of **cosmonauts**.

2 Use role-play to demonstrate a rocket in **orbit**. Discuss some synonyms for **orbit** (e.g. 'circle'; 'travel round').

Phonics

–ly suffix	finally, suddenly
–ness suffix	blackness, darkness
Longer words	adventure, everyone, happening, moving, practising, suddenly
Common exception words	again, could, even, great, hour(s), last, many, only, people, should, would

Phonics activity

How many words can the children find that use the suffix '–ed'? What tense are the words in?

2 First steps

Read the text together and then encourage the children to discuss the following questions.

1 What are the two main characters called? What are they?
Belka and Strelka. They are dogs/space dogs/ cosmonauts.

2 Where were Belka and Strelka going?
On a rocket, into space, to go into orbit.

3 When did Belka and Strelka go into space?
19th August 1960.

4 Did you like the text? Why? Why not?
Answers will vary but encourage the children to explain their answers (e.g. *I liked it but I was a bit worried about the dogs being on their own*).

3 Explore

- Belka and Strelka did not choose to go into space. Discuss whether you think they wanted to go into space. The children may make links to the first paragraph where Belka and Strelka wag their tails. Do the children think it was fair to send them into space? Why were dogs sent into space rather than humans?
- In the fourth paragraph, the author uses special language to make the reader worry about Belka and Strelka (e.g. 'But why were Belka and Strelka so still?'; 'Everyone held their breath'; 'Belka and Strelka were not moving *at all*'; 'Minutes turned into hours'). Discuss the techniques used in these sentences (e.g. the use of a question; the use of short sentences; the use of italics for emphasis). Explore reasons why you think the author decided to use language in this way. You could read on and make comparisons with the language used later in the paragraph when everyone is feeling relieved.

4 Skills focus

See pages 162 to 163

Use the information from the **Skills guide** and the relevant **Skills graphic** to introduce the skill of retrieval.

1 Model the skill using the **Unit 17 Modelling slides** and the **Modelling retrieval** guidance on page 162.

2 The children can then attempt the **Retrieval** questions on page 166.

3 Finally, the **Mix it up!** questions on page 167 offer practice in a range of comprehension skills.

Answers and marking guidance for all questions are included on pages 162 to 163.

5 Where next?

- Speaking and listening task: Belka and Strelka were not alone on their trip to space. A rabbit, 40 mice, two rats and lots of fruit flies went into space with them. Together, find out what happened to Belka and Strelka and their 'spacemates' after the end of the extract. You could do this by reading the rest of the book or by researching information from other texts or the internet. The children could work together to create a puppet show telling the story of Belka and Strelka's trip.
- Writing task: As a class, find out more about other animals that have travelled to space. The children could research and write their own fact file for other space animals. Please note: many of the animals sent up did not survive; therefore, care should be taken when researching this topic. Animals that did survive their initial flight include Able and Baker the monkeys, Ham the chimp and Felicette the cat.

Reading list

Fiction

- *The Darkest Dark* by Chris Hadfield (Linked text: Unit 16)
- *Mousetronaut* by Mark Kelly
- *The Three Little Aliens and the Big Bad Robot* by Margaret McNamara

Class reads

- *Margaret and the Moon* by Dean Robbins

Non-fiction

- *Little Kids First Big Book of Space* by Catherine D. Hughes

Poetry

- *Space Poems* by Gaby Morgan

Films

- *Space Buddies* (Walt Disney Home Entertainment, 2009)
- *Space Chimps* (Vanguard Films and Animation, 2008)

Modelling retrieval

See Unit 17 Modelling slides

Use the **Skills guide** (see pages 16 to 17) and the downloadable **Skills graphic** to support your modelling.

1 Look at the first paragraph. What were Belka and Strelka going on a mission to do?

fly all the way around/orbit the Earth

Read the question together. Model using the locator and scanning for the key word 'mission' to find the relevant information. Some children may answer 'go into space'. In this case, refocus them on the question word 'what' rather than 'where' and encourage them to reread the sentence carefully.

2 What did Belka wear?

a green spacesuit

Read the question together. This question is deceptive and appears very simple at first glance. As there is no locator, it is important to model identifying and scanning for the key words 'Belka' and 'wear'. As the text reads 'put on' rather than 'wear', you should emphasise the need to find any words relating to wearing clothes.

3 Look at the fourth paragraph. Give <u>two</u> things the ground crew did when Belka and Strelka started to move.

cheered and clapped

Read the question together and explicitly model using the locator to find the correct section. Some children may respond with the ground crew's actions from earlier in the paragraph (e.g. 'watched', 'held their breath'). In this case, refocus them on the key words 'started to move' and point out that this is an example of a question where the key words are close to but not exactly the same as the text ('started to wag'). Support the children to find the relevant sentence and choose two actions that the ground crew did ('cheered', 'clapped', 'hugged', 'cried'). Think aloud: *What did the ground crew do in this part of the paragraph?*

4 Look at the last paragraph. How many times did Belka and Strelka orbit Earth? Tick <u>one</u>.

once ☐

lots of times ☑

ten times ☐

twice ☐

Read the question together. Model locating the correct section and identifying key words within the question. Ask the children to think of different ways to say 'orbit' and scan the paragraph for those words (here, 'circled' is used). Some children may tick 'ten times' as they will equate ten with being many. If so, remind them we are retrieving information directly from the text. Think aloud: *Does the text actually say ten times?*

Retrieval questions mark scheme

See page 166

Answer	Guidance
1 (little) cosmonauts	Remind the children to use the locator to find the appropriate information. Some may find this challenging as identifying key words in the question will not necessarily support their answer here. Explain to the children that key words include synonyms and similar phrases to those in the question. **Award 1 mark for the correct answer.**
2 practising staying calm around noises/ time in special kennels on their own/ standing on a shaking platform	If the children respond very briefly (e.g. 'calm', 'kennels'), encourage them to explain their point fully using the information in the text. Some may answer vaguely (e.g. 'get used to how it would feel'). If so, explain that the question asks for two pieces of information and that they should be more specific. **Award 2 marks for 2 or more correct answers.**

Answer		Guidance
3	<table><tr><td></td><td>T</td><td>F</td></tr><tr><td>Both dogs wore green spacesuits.</td><td></td><td>✓</td></tr><tr><td>The rocket was quiet.</td><td></td><td>✓</td></tr><tr><td>Strelka wore a red spacesuit.</td><td>✓</td><td></td></tr><tr><td>The rocket shook.</td><td>✓</td><td></td></tr></table>	The children may find the second statement challenging as the text only alludes to the rocket being noisy. If they need additional support, focus them on to the sentence beginning 'The rocket shuddered …'. **Award 2 marks for all 4 statements correctly ticked. Award 1 mark for 3 statements correctly ticked.**
4	The dogs were dead/hurt/ had not survived.	Some children may try to use inference here. If they struggle, remind them that this is a retrieval question, meaning the answer is right there in the text, and encourage them to use 'Fastest finger first' (see page 17) to find the answer. **Award 1 mark for any reference to the dogs being dead, hurt or not surviving.**
5	ocean/land/space/Earth	Again, the children may need support to locate this information as the text uses 'round and round' and 'circled' rather than 'orbited'. In this case, discuss possible synonyms for 'orbited'. **Award 1 mark for 1 or more correct answers. Do not accept references to things not listed in the text (e.g. stars).**

Mix it up! questions mark scheme

See page 167

Answer		Guidance
1	noises	If the children respond with more than one word, write out the sentence for them and model removing all the words they do not need, until they are left with only one. **Award 1 mark for the correct answer. Do not accept any additional or alternative words.** Skill: Word meaning.
2	Put on their spacesuits.	The locator is hidden in this question ('there was only one thing left to do'). If the children find this challenging, explain that the first part of the question is the locator and encourage them to scan the text for that phrase. **Award 1 mark for any reference to the dogs putting on their spacesuits.** Skill: Retrieval.
3	excited/nervous	If the children provide a vague response (e.g. 'happy'), encourage them to improve their answer with synonyms. **Award 1 mark for any reference to a plausible emotion.** Skill: Inference.
4	Belka and Strelka did not move. [4] Belka and Strelka stood on a shaking platform. [2] Belka and Strelka started training. [1] Belka and Strelka's rocket launched. [3] Belka and Strelka circled the Earth. [5]	The children should be adept at sequencing by this point in the year; however, some may still benefit from being given cut-up sections of the story and completing this as a physical ordering exercise first. You could also support them to highlight and number the different sections. **Award 1 mark for the correct numbers in at least 3 boxes and 2 marks for the correct numbers in all boxes.** Skill: Sequencing.
5	Belka and Strelka will get home safely and have lots of yummy food.	Predictions could be positive or negative. Encourage the children to verbally justify their prediction using the text. Once completed, share the ending to the story. Think aloud: *Were our predictions correct? Why? Why not?* **Award 1 mark for a plausible prediction.** Skill: Prediction.

Dogs in Space, by Vix Southgate

Dogs in Space is the story of two special dogs called Belka and Strelka. These two famous dogs travelled all the way into space and became SPACE DOGS!

Belka and Strelka were going to be ... SPACE DOGS. Belka and Strelka were going on a special mission to space, to fly all the way around the Earth – a journey called an orbit. They seemed to know something exciting was happening. They wagged their tails; they were ready to start training straight away.

The two little cosmonauts needed to get used to how it would feel inside the rocket. Some of the exercises were: practising staying calm with loud noises around them; spending time in special kennels to get used to being on their own away from people; and standing on a platform that shook under their paws. They practised again and again, until they were finally ready for their mission. There was only one thing left to do: put on their special doggy spacesuits – a red one for Strelka and a green one for Belka.

Launch Day 19 August 1960. Finally, the big day arrived. The rocket stood on the launch pad ready for blast-off. Belka and Strelka were ready too. The rocket shuddered, shook, rumbled and roared ... then broke free and soared into the sky! Up and up it went through the clouds until it reached space. Belka and Strelka's great adventure had begun!

All was still and quiet as Belka and Strelka began their orbit. The ground crew watched on their television monitors. Everything was working as it should. But why were Belka and Strelka so still? Everyone held their breath. Belka and Strelka were not moving *at all.*

Minutes turned into hours. It was feared the brave little space dogs had not survived the launch. Then suddenly someone thought they saw Belka wriggle. Could it be? Yes! And then Strelka started to wag her tail and bark! The team cheered and clapped and hugged each other. Some even cried with joy and relief. Belka and Strelka were ALIVE!

Round and round the Earth they flew. They saw the blue of the oceans and the greens and browns of the land shining against the blackness of space. Not even a human had seen such sights! Belka and Strelka circled the Earth many times until, at last, it was time to go home.

Retrieval

Name: ______________________________

1 Look at the first sentence of the second paragraph. What does the author call Belka and Strelka?

______________________________ 1 mark

2 How were the dogs trained? Give **two** ways.

1. ______________________________

2. ______________________________ 2 marks

3 Look at the second and third paragraphs. Tick to show whether each statement is true or false.

	True	**False**
Both dogs wore green spacesuits.		
The rocket was quiet.		
Strelka wore a red spacesuit.		
The rocket shook.		

2 marks

4 Look at the fourth paragraph. What did the ground crew think had happened to Belka and Strelka?

____

______________________________ 1 mark

5 What did Belka and Strelka see while they orbited?

____

______________________________ 1 mark

Mix it up!

Name: ______________________

1 Look at the sentence beginning *Some of the exercises were ... .* Find and copy **one** word that means the same as 'sounds'.

____

1 mark

2 There was only one thing left for the dogs to do after practising. What was it?

____

____

1 mark

3 Look at the third paragraph. How do you think the ground crew felt when the rocket launched?

____

1 mark

4 Number the events to show the order in which they happened in the text. One has been done for you.

Belka and Strelka did not move.	☐
Belka and Strelka stood on a shaking platform.	2
Belka and Strelka started training.	☐
Belka and Strelka's rocket launched.	☐
Belka and Strelka circled the Earth.	☐

2 marks

5 What do you think will happen next to Belka and Strelka?

____

____

____

1 mark

A Bottle of Happiness

by Pippa Goodhart

Printable text • Modelling slides Photocopiable text and questions • pages 172 to 175

Celebrating the diversity of different cultures and groups is just as important as recognising the value of an individual. This text explores the lessons that people with very different backgrounds and lifestyles can teach one another. The text used in Progress check 3, *Ossiri and the Bala Mengro*, looks at similar themes. You may wish to discuss the similarities and differences between the two texts once the Progress check has been completed.

1 Get ready

Discuss the **Key vocabulary** identified in the **Language toolkit** and then complete the vocabulary and phonics activities as desired. Please note that the selected vocabulary is a guide. Depending on the needs of your cohort, additional vocabulary discussion may be beneficial before, during and after reading. Next, display the text (pages 172 to 173) so the children can see the title and any illustrations, and encourage the children to discuss the following questions before reading.

1 Look at the title. What do you think might happen in this story?
The children should be able to make simple predictions based on the title (e.g. *There's going to be a bottle that someone uses to make someone happy, so it could be an adventure*).

2 What makes you happy? Why?
Answers will vary. Try to encourage all the children to contribute to the discussion.

3 Do you like to tell stories? Which stories do you know by heart?
Answers will vary. Encourage the children to tell their partner a story. If some struggle to remember a story, remind them of traditional tales they should know, for example 'Hansel and Gretel' from Unit 11.

4 Do you think stories make people happy? Why?
Answers will vary. Hopefully the majority of the children will give a positive response. Encourage them to share stories that have made them happy.

Language toolkit

Key vocabulary

enough	exchange	existed
mined	nothing	poor
silence	stallholder	stopper

Vocabulary discussion questions

- What can be **poor**?
- What things do you have **enough** of?
- Can you think of a time when you did an **exchange** with someone?
- Can you explain the difference between quiet and **silence**?

Vocabulary activities

1 The word **nothing** begins with the letter string 'no–'. Can the children make a list of other words that start like this? What do these words have in common?

2 **Stallholder** is a compound word. How many other compound words can the children think of?

Phonics

–er suffix	richer
–ful suffix	beautiful
Longer words	happiness, something, stallholder, together
Common exception words	again, beautiful, because, child, climbed, even, find, many, people, poor, told, whole

Phonics activity

How many different words can the children find that contain the suffixes '–ing', '–ed' or '–ly'?

2 First steps

Read the text together and then encourage the children to discuss the following questions.

1 **There are two different groups of people who live on the mountain. What is different about them?**
One side is rich and works all the time to get richer – they catch fish, mine jewels and grow crops. They sell things in their market. The other side is poor – they work hard but their crops don't grow very well. They share things and love to share stories. Some children may need support to locate this information or give additional detail.

2 **What is the main character called? Which other characters appear in the story?**
Pim. Other characters include Tiddle the dog, stallholders at the market and Uncle Freddie.

3 **Where does Pim travel to at the start of the text?**
Pim goes to the other side of the mountain. Some children may respond that he travelled to the market; in this case, refocus them on the phrase 'start of the text'.

4 **Did you like the text? Why? Why not?**
Answers will vary but encourage the children to explain their answers (e.g. *I liked it because Pim went on an adventure*).

3 Explore

- This story is a folk tale that has a moral message. Discuss other folk tales the children may have read, especially those from other cultures (e.g. 'King Midas', 'The Hare and the Tortoise'). What is the message in each of these stories? You could discuss whether it is similar or different to the message in *A Bottle of Happiness*.
- What words and phrases does the author use to compare and contrast the two groups of people on the two sides of the mountain? Discuss how each group of people is described. You could also discuss which vocabulary is repeated (e.g. 'worked hard'; 'grew' and 'grew less well'). To aid your discussion, you could work as a class to show this contrasting language in a table.
- Discuss what the positives and negatives would be of living on each side of the mountain. Which side of the mountain would the children like to live on, and why?
- The author uses words such as 'the other side', 'your people' and 'your happiness'. Discuss how the author uses words like this to make the two groups seem different to one another. Does this language make the children think the two groups are happy to see each other, or are they suspicious of each other?

4 Skills focus

See pages 170 to 171

Use the information from the **Skills guide** and the relevant **Skills graphic** to introduce the skill of inference.

1 Model the skill using the **Unit 18 Modelling slides** and the **Modelling inference** guidance on page 170.

2 The children can then attempt the **Inference** questions on page 174.

3 Finally, the **Mix it up!** questions on page 175 offer practice in a range of comprehension skills.

Answers and marking guidance for all questions are included on pages 170 to 171.

5 Where next?

- Speaking and listening task: Set up a class link to a school in another country. The British Council's 'Connecting Classrooms' programme is a great way to do this. The children share their experiences of everyday life with children who live somewhere different and celebrate what joins them together.
- Writing task: Support the children to research life in a different city or country. They could write a presentation about the similarities and differences between their lives and the lives of children in other countries. This could be used to highlight what we have in common as well as what makes each country or culture special. This activity could be linked to the task above.

Reading list

Fiction

- *All the Colors of the Earth* by Sheila Hamanaka
- *Ossiri and the Bala Mengro* by Richard O'Neill and Katharine Quarmby (Linked text: Progress check 3)
- *Whoever You Are* by Mem Fox

Class reads

- *This Is How We Do It* by Matt Lamothe
- *Welcome to Our World: A Celebration of Children Everywhere!* by Moira Butterfield

Non-fiction

- *At the Same Moment, Around the World* by Clotilde Perrin
- *How to Tell a Story* by Daniel Nayeri

Poetry

- *Over the Hills and Far Away: A Treasury of Nursery Rhymes from Around the World* by Elizabeth Hammill

Modelling inference

See Unit 18 Modelling slides

Use the **Skills guide** (see pages 20 to 21) and the downloadable **Skills graphic** to support your modelling.

1 **Look at the sentence beginning *The people on the other side of the mountain …* . Do you think these people were happy? Tick one. Explain your answer.**

Yes ☐ No ☑

No – because their crops do not grow well.

Read the question together. Model using the locator and identifying and scanning the text for the key words to find clues. Continue by having a class vote to decide whether the people were happy. Think aloud: *Let's vote – are they happy?* Discuss the verdict, using the text. Repeat the process for the opposite opinion, emphasising that both opinions are valid but it's important we give reasons from the text. However, point out that the question requires only one opinion.

2 **Why do you think Pim wanted to find a new story?**

He was bored with hearing the same stories.

Read the question together. As there is no locator, model using the key words 'find a new story' to scan for the appropriate section. Then model reading around the key words to look for clues. Discuss the sentence 'they told the same stories over and over again'. Think aloud: *How would Pim feel about this? How would his feelings encourage him to find a new story?*

3 ***"I haven't got anything," said Pim.* How do you think Pim was feeling at this point in the story? Why?**

He was surprised because he did not have anything to give in exchange.

Read the question together and begin by pointing out that it asks for two pieces of information – a feeling and a reason why. Model using the locator to find the appropriate section in the text. The children are likely to decide on a feeling relatively easily, but may struggle to give a reason. Think aloud: *Imagine you are Pim – how would you feel if you wanted to buy something but had no money?* Discuss the possible reasons behind Pim's feelings such as his being confused because his people always shared everything.

4 **What was in Pim's bottle at the end of the text? Explain why.**

It was empty because happiness can't be bottled.

Read the question together. As with **Modelling question 3** above, point out that it is asking for an answer and a reason. This is a challenging question and is good preparation for Key Stage 2. You could explain that this question would be worth 2 marks. The children are likely to require some support to fully explain their answer. You could begin a discussion about Pim's empty bottle, encouraging the children to discuss possible reasons such as the fact that happiness can't be used to buy things and that people have to feel it for themselves.

Inference questions mark scheme

See page 174

	Answer	Guidance
1	No – the rich people didn't share stories. *OR* Yes – they could catch fish/mine valuable jewels, so they were never hungry.	Your previous modelling of **Modelling question 1** will be helpful here. Some children may still need support to examine the clues in the text. You could encourage them to look again at the descriptions of the two groups of people in the first paragraph. **Award 1 mark for a plausible explanation.**
2	excited/thrilled	If some children respond with very simple emotions (e.g. 'happy'), encourage them to widen their vocabulary choice. You could use one of the vocabulary activities on page 15 to help with this. **Award 1 mark for any reference to a plausible positive emotion. Accept negative emotions (e.g. worried) if the children can adequately explain why, using the text.**

Answer	Guidance
3 smile ✓ laugh ✓	If necessary, remind the children to 'tick two' for this question. If they answer 'shout', refocus them on the word 'probably' and encourage them to reread the paragraph and consider what Pim was likely to have done. **Award 1 mark for the correct answers ticked.**
4 They were in a rush to go back to the market/to get the fruit.	If the children answer vaguely (e.g. 'they were in a rush'), remind them to explain why using details from the text. **Award 1 mark for any reference to a plausible explanation.**
5 surprised because he thought he had managed to collect happiness and laughter from his side of the mountain	Many children will supply Pim's emotion with ease. If they struggle to give a reason, ask them to read the previous paragraph and pretend to be Pim – how would they feel? Why? **Award 1 mark for a plausible emotion and 1 mark for a plausible reason.**

Mix it up! questions mark scheme

See page 175

Answer	Guidance
1 a market ✓ the sea ✓	The children may need reminding to tick two options. The distractors are all present in the story, so close reading is important. If necessary, encourage the children to begin by removing the options they know are incorrect before rereading the first paragraph closely to find the answers. **Award 1 mark for the correct answers ticked.** Skill: Retrieval.
2 over and over again *OR* over and over *OR* told the same stories over and over again	If the children struggle, encourage them to locate the correct sentence and then remove any words that are not needed. **Award 1 mark for a correct answer. Accept any relevant phrases. Do not accept one-word answers or the whole sentence.** Skill: Word meaning.
3 He looked down at the market./ He went to the market.	Some responses may use information from later in the paragraph (e.g. 'he tried to buy fruit') or from later paragraphs. In both cases, remind children to use the locator to find the appropriate section of the text. **Award 1 mark for any reference to looking down at the market or going to the market.** Skill: Sequencing.
4 Go away! You've got nothing in the bottle.	This is the first time children have encountered this question type. If necessary, encourage them to role-play the conversation between the stallholder and Pim in small groups. **Award 1 mark for a plausible phrase (either direct or reported speech).** Skill: Inference.
5 Pim will go back and try to bottle happiness again.	If necessary, encourage the children to reread the final paragraph and put themselves in Pim's shoes. **Award 1 mark for a plausible prediction.** Skill: Prediction.

A Bottle of Happiness, by Pippa Goodhart

This is an extract from a story about the people on two sides of a mountain. One side of the mountain is rich and people work to get richer, while the other side is poor but full of laughter.

There was once a big mountain. The people on one side of the mountain caught fish and mined jewels and grew crops. They were rich, and they worked hard at getting richer. They had a big market where they sold things to each other. The people on the other side of the mountain worked hard too, but their soil was poor, so crops grew less well. They had no sea to fish in or jewels to mine. They grew and made just enough for them all to eat and wear if they shared things. Because they lived together, they loved sharing stories too. They told the same stories over and over again.

But, one day, a child called Pim said, "I want to find a new story. I'm going over the mountain to see what's on the other side." So Pim and Tiddle the dog climbed right up to the top of the mountain. Then they looked down and saw ... "Wow, look at that, Tiddle!" said Pim. Pim and Tiddle ran down to the market. There was more there than Pim had known even existed in the whole world! Pim asked a stallholder, "Please may I eat one of those beautiful fruits?"

"What will you give me in return for the fruit?" said the man.

"I haven't got anything," said Pim.

"There must be something that your people have that we don't," said a woman. Pim looked at the market people.

"I think we have more happiness than you do," said Pim.

"Bring us some of that, then," said the man.

So Pim walked back over the mountain, thinking about how to carry happiness. I'll catch some laughter, thought Pim. "Uncle Freddie, please will you sing for us?" said Pim. Uncle Freddie sang and Tiddle danced. People laughed. Pim carefully caught laughter in a bottle. Some music and love slipped in with it. Pim put the stopper into the bottle to stop the happiness from leaking out. Then Pim and Tiddle ran with the bottle of happiness back over the mountain. It was light to carry.

"Here's some happiness," said Pim, offering the bottle.

"Open it up," said the woman. "I need to see how good your happiness is before I know how many fruits to exchange for it."

"It's really good," said Pim. "It's got laughing and music and love in it."

Pim pulled the stopper from the bottle. Pim tipped the bottle to pour out the happiness, but what came out was ... silence and nothing to see.

Inference

Name: ______________________

1 Do you think the rich people were happier than the people on the other side of the mountain? Tick **one**.

Yes ☐ No ☐

Why?

____

____ 1 mark

2 How do you think Pim and Tiddle felt when they set off to climb the mountain?

____ 1 mark

3 Look at the paragraph beginning *So Pim walked back …* . What things did Pim probably do when he was back on his side of the mountain? Tick **two**.

smile ☐ cry ☐ shout ☐ laugh ☐ 1 mark

4 *Then Pim and Tiddle ran with the bottle of happiness back over the mountain.* Why do you think Pim and Tiddle **ran** back?

____

____ 1 mark

5 *… silence and nothing to see.*
How do you think Pim felt when he opened the bottle? Why?

He felt ______________________ because

____

____ 2 marks

Mix it up!

Name: ______________________

1 Look at the first paragraph. What did the rich side of the mountain have? Tick **two**.

a market ☐

poor soil ☐

the sea ☐

stories ☐

1 mark

2 Look at the first paragraph. Find and copy **a group of words** that tells us the stories were told lots of times.

____

1 mark

3 Look at the second paragraph. What did Pim do after he got to the top of the mountain?

____

____

1 mark

4 What do you think the stallholder might say at the end of the story? Write your answer in the speech bubble.

____

____

____

1 mark

5 What do you think Pim will do next?

____

____

1 mark

Ossiri and the Bala Mengro

by Richard O'Neill and Katharine Quarmby

Printable text   Photocopiable text and questions • pages 177 to 179

This extract is from a story about a traveller girl called Ossiri who creates her own musical instrument, the Tattin Django. Ossiri ventures into the hills to practise, ignoring her family's warnings about the fearsome ogre, the Bala Mengro. Written by Richard O'Neill and Katharine Quarmby, two Romani authors, this story is a wonderful celebration of traveller life and culture. This text and *A Bottle of Happiness* (Unit 18) focus on celebrating different people and cultures. After this Progress check is completed, you could spend some time to making links between the two texts, sharing their similarities and differences. **For guidance on running this task, see page 11.**

Progress check questions mark scheme

Answer	Guidance
1 scared/curious	Some children may make deeper inferences (e.g. 'she doesn't care'). In this case, ask them to check their understanding (e.g. she only cares about playing her instrument). If necessary, ask the children to put themselves in Ossiri's position. How would they feel if they were living near a monster? Why? Some children may be able to justify their response using the text (e.g. 'She feels curious, because she's never seen a monster before'). **Award 1 mark for any reference to a plausible emotion.** Skill: Inference.
2 Ossiri's family arrived at the camping ground. [1] Ossiri talked to a girl. [4] Ossiri's family had a meal. [3] Ossiri's family built a fire. [2]	If necessary, encourage the children to identify one key word for each statement and then scan the text for them to help them order the events. **Award 1 mark for the correct numbers in all boxes.** Skill: Sequencing.
3 She promised not to go into the hills alone.	If the children refer to the monster, prompt them to reread the section and tell them that this is a retrieval question. What does the text actually say? Ask them to use 'fastest finger first' (see page 17) to prove their answer. **Award 1 mark for the correct answer.** Skill: Retrieval.
4 gigantic *OR* huge	Previously we have accepted more than one word, but children should now be more comfortable with the 'find and copy' question type. **Award 1 mark for a correct answer. Do not accept answers of more than one word, even if the correct word is included (e.g. 'gigantic yawn' or 'huge monster'). If necessary, remind the children how to answer 'find and copy' questions.** Skill: Word meaning.
5 Ossiri goes home. [✓]	This prediction requires some quite complex inference and understanding. If the children find it difficult, take away an incorrect option to provide less challenge. You may wish to discuss each option together or ask the children who respond incorrectly to explain their prediction to help you to ascertain their level of understanding. **Award 1 mark for the correct answer ticked.** Skill: Prediction.

Progress check 3

Name: ____________________

1 How do you think Ossiri felt when the girl told her about the Bala Mengro?

____________________ 1 mark

2 Look at the first section. Number the events to show the order in which they happened in the story. One has been done for you.

Ossiri's family arrived at the camping ground. [1]

Ossiri talked to a girl. [ ]

Ossiri's family had a meal. [ ]

Ossiri's family built a fire. [ ]

1 mark

3 Look at the section beginning *Ossiri joined her family ...* . What did Ossiri promise her father?

____

____________________ 1 mark

4 *The sound echoed off the hillside. As she paused for breath she heard a gigantic yawn. Ossiri looked around and saw a dark opening in the hillside, and at the entrance a huge monster.*
Find and copy **one** word that means the same as 'large'.

____________________ 1 mark

5 Which of these events is most likely to happen next? Tick **one**.

Ossiri plays her instrument again. [ ]

Ossiri goes home. [ ]

The Bala Mengro starts singing. [ ]

The Bala Mengro captures Ossiri. [ ]

1 mark

Ossiri and the Bala Mengro, by Richard O'Neill and Katharine Quarmby

This is an extract from a story about a young girl, Ossiri, who loves to play her Tattin Django, a homemade musical instrument that makes a very loud noise. Her family does not like the sound, so whenever she can, Ossiri slips away to practise it.

After a long journey the family arrived at their new camping ground. They built a fire and cooked an evening meal. Ossiri moved away from the fireside and started to play quietly. One of the farmer's daughters heard her and put her hands over her ears. "You don't want to play that around here. If you wake the great ogre you'll be in terrible trouble."

"What's that?" asked Ossiri.

"A huge hairy monster, as tall as a barn. It lives in the cave up there." The girl pointed up the steep hillside. "It loves its sleep and woe betide anyone who wakes it." She shivered. "Last week my father was ploughing the field next to the ogre's cave and the jangling of the harness and the plough blades cutting through the stony soil woke the ogre up. It chased him for hours across hill and dale. That ogre chases anyone who wakes it."

"What would it have done if it had caught him?" asked Ossiri.

"You don't want to know!" said the girl, and walked away.

Ossiri joined her family at the fireside and told them about the ogre.

"Oh Dordi," exclaimed her father. "I didn't know the Bala Mengro was still here. You must be careful." Ossiri promised that she would never go into the hills alone. But she couldn't resist the chance to practise. The very next day she took her Tattin Django into the peaks. The sound echoed off the hillside. As she paused for breath she heard a gigantic yawn. Ossiri looked around and saw a dark opening in the hillside, and at the entrance a huge monster. It was the Bala Mengro – rubbing its large, red eyes. Ossiri wanted to run but her legs were frozen to the spot.

"I was asleep till you came along!" the Bala Mengro boomed. It was huge, and as hairy as a Shire horse.

"Sorry," Ossiri trembled, shaking from her head to her toes. "I won't wake you again. Please let me go."

"No," growled the Bala Mengro. "You must play for me again!"

Shocked, Ossiri played as loud as she could. The Bala Mengro rumbled, deep and loud. It was singing! The hills shook as the great ogre started to dance.

Eventually, the Bala Mengro stopped dancing and disappeared inside the cave. Ossiri began to tiptoe away, her face white with fear, but she felt its grip on her shoulder. Ossiri froze, but the Bala Mengro just dropped a heavy chain into her hand and walked away.

Discover *Complete Comprehension* for Year 1

Unit	Target skill	Title	Author	Genre
1	Inference	Starting School	Jo Gray	Picture
2	Retrieval	Our Senses	Jo Gray	Picture
3	Retrieval	Mary Had a Little Lamb	Sarah Josepha Hale	Poetry
4	Word meaning	Jack and Jill	Traditional	Poetry
5	Inference	Snow Bear	Tony Mitton	Fiction
6	Word meaning	Can't You Sleep, Little Bear?	Martin Waddell	Fiction
7	Inference	Little Red	Jo Gray	Fiction
8	Retrieval	Wolves	James Maclaine	Non-fiction
9	Sequencing	The Three Little Pigs	Jo Gray	Fiction
10	Inference	The Three Little Pigs (Revolting Rhymes)	Roald Dahl	Poetry
11	Word meaning	Looking After Rabbits	Fiona Patchett	Non-fiction
12	Prediction	The Pet	Tony Bradman	Poetry
13	Inference	Chocolate Cake	Michael Rosen	Poetry
14	Sequencing	Chocolate Cake Recipe	Jo Gray	Non-fiction
15	Word meaning	Plant Facts	Izzi Howell	Non-fiction
16	Retrieval	Jack and the Beanstalk	Jo Gray	Fiction
17	Inference	My Two Grannies	Floella Benjamin	Fiction
18	Word meaning	Grandad Mandela	Zazi, Ziwelene and Zindzi Mandela	Non-fiction
Progress check 1	Mixed skills	Bee Frog	Martin Waddell	Fiction
Progress check 2	Mixed skills	You Can't Take an Elephant on the Bus	Patricia Cleveland-Peck	Fiction
Progress check 3	Mixed skills	Seaside Towns	Claire Hibbert	Non-fiction

Schofield&Sims

For further information and to place your order visit
www.schofieldandsims.co.uk or telephone 01484 607080